DisHarmony:
A Jigsaw
Collection of
Misguided Dating

DisHarmony:
A Jigsaw
Collection of
Misguided Dating

Rachel R. Kovach

Library of Congress Control Number:		2020909350
ISBN:	Hardcover	978-1-9845-8070-2
	Softcover	978-1-9845-8069-6
	eBook	978-1-9845-8068-9

Print information available on the last page.

Rev. date: 05/21/2020

To order additional copies of this book, contact:
Xlibris
1-888-795-4274
www.Xlibris.com
Orders@Xlibris.com
813573

Dedicated to Joe and Renee and John and Rosie
for setting the highest expectations for a lifelong partner
and teaching so many how to love for eternity.

Dedicated to my partner in life,
wherever you may be.
I love you, and I am praying for you
until I am yours.

Racklee

CONTENTS

I: A Beginning to Every Story

Getting to know another human being in our time has become quite the feat. What was once a simple concept has produced novels, television shows, therapies, and religions that help our fearful selves explore the concept of attaching to another person, another life, or another path. One hundred years ago, courting rituals included arranged dinners by parental units to see if compatibility was possible. Examples of youthful rebellion included sneaking off to a speakeasy and dancing in underground jazz clubs, which allowed many to interact, discover passion, and stumble into love. Sixty years ago, couples settled in the sharing of pins, jackets, and rings to display their love for one another. A boom in hedonistic ideals such as free love and polygamy provided a needed shake-up to mainstream dating culture in order for humanity to grow and evolve.

As the decades have fallen together in a heap of pop culture and movie quotes, our society has become more dependent on the use of technology to help us communicate. Our lives have become reliant on instant gratification—having what we want when we want it rather than working hard to build a foundation that will see us through the most trying of hardships. The technology era has become useful in helping the overscheduled find time for social interactions and dalliances of love without the burden of long-term commitment and follow-through. With the click of a button and the swipe of a finger, humans are able to share interests and dreams with one another using multiple interfaces for desired image distribution.

I myself have wandered the crooked path of love through many friend suggestions, endless apps, and cliché websites that promise everlasting love, companionship, and laughter with the enlistment of my membership and credit-card information. While I avoided the corny commercials and adorable advertisements that spammed my digital mailboxes, I eventually catered to their temptations and enjoyed multiple six- to twelve-month explorations of the dating world. While none of the gentlemen I encountered became my true match in life, I could argue that I gained more lessons about the ways of our age with them than I had while seeking my bachelor's, master's, and doctoral degrees.

It is an interesting dating era in which we live. Currently, the battle lines for dating decorum are completely blurred. Previous societal and gender roles, while not necessarily accurate in depicting the traits of every individual, provided structure and formula. These courting rituals were followed to find a long-term companion, lover, and match. Yet as my array of dating experiences has proven, those rules and standards are obsolete and disregarded. There isn't an exact science to meeting the right person. It requires men to jump through a multitude of hoops to effectively and appropriately engage with women, and it requires women to be constantly analyzing and adjusting their standards and expectations—all while taking the perfect selfie. While these pieces are continuously evolving, there are higher occurrences of miscommunication, missed opportunities, and dismissed engagements.

From my varied experiences, I have always found comfort in order and purpose. When I reflected on the ups and tumbling downs of dating, I realized that many of the lessons I learned began being categorized in an alphabetical fashion. While the perfectionist in me would like to present my readers with the exact alphabet as to why the dating experience is such a hot mess, I truly don't have all the answers or experiences I need to formulate those letters. I may stumble upon those letters in my future; it just depends on who wanders into my path next.

These stories are for many audiences, for those seeking comedy within a topic that produces many emotions of dissatisfaction and awkwardness, and for the bleeding heart that lives to find their happily ever after only to find their heart crumbling as another holiday passes by without their significant other in sight. This is an account of the many lessons and stories that paved the imperfect path of love in which I wandered, and I do wish that my experiences bring you laughter, wisdom, and hope.

II: APRIL'S FOOL

I'm terrified.
My bones are stiffening
Muscles locking into a fearful rigidity
I can feel the increasing pressure of air in my body gripping my
internal organs with the fiercest grip.
April is approaching.

Thirty days didn't used to be so daunting
So horrific
So spine chilling
Yet as it approaches,
The frozen castle protecting my heart is securing its defenses
My ribs are coated with a tempered resin,
A security blanket that protects my lungs through the month
long storm,
For I will be holding my breath more often than not to survive.

April's weapons are cruel and calculating,
The attacks are silent and come without warning,
I should have learned, I should be better
Each memory a tainted poison that coats her daggers for long
term suffering
She seems to improve her tactics as the years have past.

The memories of loss and failure are ever present,
The life I wanted, the ones I needed,
Now transformed into dust, into pain, into isolation,
I can't silence the scream that sends vibrations through my blood,
Ghosts of the missing place their hands upon my throat,
Surrendering to the pain would give her another win,
My pride cannot let that be.

Other months have granted me courage and strength,
I could almost forget that I shall face the fourth month again.
The warmth of the summer melts the fortress trapping my spirit,
Fall's changing colors remind me to forgive,
The winter allows for hope and possibilities to reignite my passions and daydream for what can be,
Yet it is spring that betrays me,
For April is ready.

The torment never ceases
April is constant
The mocking flower blossoms evidence of her victory,
My tears and blood the nutrients that allow her spoils to thrive

What fool would volunteer to be by my side though this battle?
I can't blame them for walking away
For we all have ghosts to reckon with
I am prepared to battle April once again,
My right hand aching for another to be beside it in a war with no end

III: Blind Dating

Creatures of habit enjoy their routines by the nature of their title alone. They will typically rise to the day within the same hour window, roll to their preferred side, stretch the opposite leg that fell asleep during their night of tossing and turning, discover the internal discipline within themselves to sit up to the side of the bed, place their feet upon the floor in a count of three, and progress through the navigation of their day. These poster children of predisposition will enter their favorite café and communicate repetitive pleasantries and daily banter without saying a word of their order because the barista started developing their beverage from the moment they heard the daily patron's vehicle pull up to their unspoken-but-agreed-upon parking spot. This is a session that lasts thirty to sixty minutes, depending on the day of the week that it occurs, and then the consumer drinks their coffee and strategizes how to conquer the obstacles and changes that will most likely alter their daily tasks.

It is because of this need for order, which is found inside the very fibers of their muscle tissues and skeletal forms, that blind dates are tsunamis that crash upon the shoreline of structure's paradise. The lack of control and the fearful residual effects of the approaching shadowed encounter leave the planned participant riddled with crazed "w" questions that haunt the mind. *Who is he? What does he do? Where did we agree to meet? Why did I say yes? What if this blind date is just the Grim Reaper's opportunity of arranging my scheduled murder?* While it may sound like I am exaggerating, this storm of questions flooded my mind when I agreed to meet him, the single highway-patrol officer who loved coffee and beagles as much as I did—that is, according to his mother.

You see, I have fallen prey to my routine and stumbled into my favorite café on a sunshine-filled Friday when, to my surprise, I did not have to work. *It's a day to rest*, according to my supervisor. In hindsight, it was his unofficial way of scheduling an extra day in Palm Springs for a poker tournament; however, I was not going to argue with the opportunity for some extra time for myself. After going through my morning routine within my studio and harnessing my beagle for a slower stroll to our coffee shop instead of driving Tucker, my '97 baby-blue Ford Explorer Sport, we made our way to our daily location and took a seat in the outdoor patio to enjoy our coffee and complimentary dog biscuits.

As I sat upon the outdoor furniture, my legs stretched upon the empty chair to my right side and my mind lost in the world of romance and historical fiction that was developed by the genius mind of Diana Gabaldon, I heard a crash within the shop and saw a woman bending down to pick up the broken pieces of her ceramic mug. My beagle, ever at the defense of all humans, began baying in protection for the fallen woman, and I went inside to help her. As I helped her collect herself, the woman wiped away her tears of embarrassment, and I assured her that klutzy behavior is a part of the human condition. She laughed at my compassionate attempt at humor, and I guided her to the nearest chair, where the barista provided her with a replacement cup of coffee for her struggles. After I mentally assessed the woman's ability to be functional without my support, I walked back to my patio haven, ready to return to the adventure that Gabaldon had led me down before the crash.

While I may have been of the belief that the woman was ready to be alone, she did not share my same opinion. She followed me to my seat and occupied the chair where my relaxed legs had been. My legs were burning with envy of the aged woman as they fell into the ninety-degree position that sitting upright dictated. The woman then began asking a series of questions that left me feeling interrogated

Rachel R. Kovach

by the finest of detectives rather than a fragile woman in her late sixties who awkwardly spilled her coffee just moments ago. After inevitably sharing my life history and, oddly, the history of my dog, she came to the conclusion that I needed to date her son. I laughed awkwardly at the sudden proposal of forced companionship; however, she assured me that she would arrange everything. According to my new companion, her son was a handsome highway-patrol officer who was in desperate need of female companionship. Her fear of being left without grandchildren crippled her heart and her fractured relationship with her son. She wanted one more attempt at finding love for her beautiful boy.

I made eye contact with the barista in an attempt for getting a lifeline. She only found my predicament humorous and suggested us meeting at the coffee shop the next morning. Lost in a lagoon of social appropriateness, I inevitably agreed to the encounter with this man for the next morning. From what I have gained from my meeting with the loving mother, her son was a highway patrolman who liked coffee and dogs. The picture she showed me of him had awkward lighting, and I couldn't gather the details of his face—only the fact that he was tall and he drove an orange muscle car with blue stripes. Oh and his name, but you don't need to know that for this story to be just as inevitably chaotic.

It was with those details that I waited for him at the shop exactly twenty-four hours later. When I entered the establishment, the mischievous barista was giggling with my drink, which was ready to be consumed and was to act as a peace offering. "She paid for it after you left yesterday," she told me as I took a sip of the tangible incentive. I discussed my escape route in the likely chance I would need to leave this forced entanglement. The barista laughed at my anxious spirit and told me it would work out the way it should. I shook my head and took a seat in the corner, where I had visual access to the door and to my barista. The plan was set. I would give this man thirty minutes of my time, have the barista text me to check on our status, and then have her call me as my loving Aunt Grace who desperately needed my help at home because her cat got trapped in her gutter. I took a breath and looked out the window, ready to meet this puzzle piece of a stranger.

Ten minutes later, I heard the deep rumblings of a V8 engine. He had arrived. He walked into the establishment in a pair of nicely worn light-wash jeans and a gray Henley sweater, and his piercing green eyes took me by surprise. He asked the barista for me by my full name, and I stood up too straight for comfort, ready to shake the hand of the handsome stranger who came to this coffee shop, which was too small for his large frame. Instead of shaking my hand, he pulled me in for a hug, and I was greeted by the smell of ocean and motor oil—a lethal combination for my hormone-driven mind. He brought me a bouquet of daisies, and I smiled at the gesture. He took a seat across from mine, and we began introducing ourselves to each other, my worries and concerns melting away with each passing comment. I didn't even feel the timed SOS text sent by my coffee-creating partner in this blind-date adventure, who caught sight of the high tides that this date would fall victim to before I got dragged under the currents of regret.

I had just finished talking about my odd fascination with Orchard Supply Hardware when I caught sight of the layer of tears in his eyes. Full of remorse, he whispered, "I'm so sorry. I can't do this."

"Do what?" I asked in confusion.

"Be here with you. I'm still in love with my wife."

A bucket of ice washed over me as my relaxed form tightened, my hands holding on to my coffee cup to keep from gripping my own legs in pain. "Your wife?"

"I'm getting divorced. Surely my mother told you?"

"No," I whispered unintentionally aggressively. "No, she did not. She mentioned that you were single and in desperate need to produce children."

"Of course she did," he said, pulling his hand away from mine. "My wife and I are going through some hard times, you know? I mean, I could change. So what that I found her in bed with my best friend? Those are issues we can work out, right?"

My eyebrows went straight up to my scalp in utter confusion with the words that escaped this handsome oddball. "Seriously?" I asked in complete shock.

"Yes, and she promised she would stop dealing drugs with him. It's my fault for introducing her to him at my high-school reunion. He does have a tendency of sleeping with the women in my life."

"Really?" I asked with fake interest.

"Yes. There was Rita and Joanne, Becky, Martha, and even Aileen. I just can't believe he would do this with my wife. We've been married for eight months! That means something, you know?"

Morbid curiosity won out, and I was already down this path before it even started. "Just to fulfill a sense of continuity, where did you meet your wife?" I asked.

"Strip club in Vegas. We got married by an Elvis. It was the perfect wedding," he replied, his eyes full of love and admiration for the woman currently screwing his best friend.

I could feel my reproductive organs building a fortress of stone to keep the potential diseases and infections this man could have on him from his promiscuous wife. The level of blind stupidity was just too much for my mind to wrap itself around. I tried to look at my lifeline, but the barista was nowhere in sight. She was sitting on the floor and in a fit of painful laughter for the torture I was enduring.

Taking a breath and conjuring the strength to develop some form of compassionate response, I grabbed his hand and said, "Well, if you believe you two are meant to be, I think you should go after her."

He looked at our joined hands and then looked into my eyes. I could see the gold flecks that were scattered within the green. He gripped my hand just a little bit tighter and began to lean in for a kiss. His lips latched on to mine in full force, my body growing rigid with surprise. The shock was so strong that my lips could not and would not cooperate with his prodding tongue, which was seeking entrance. After fifteen seconds of utter oddness, he looked up at me and shook his head. "God, you're an amazing kisser with a great rack. But I really love my wife."

A gasp of horror and laughter escaped me and the barista behind the counter. With no concrete thought or reason, I said, "Well, go after her!"

"What?" he asked.

"That's what all women want, right?" I asked with insincere intentions. "She wants you to fight for her. Go. Go get your wife back."

"I will!" he yelled, getting up from the chair and gathering his items. "You sure you're okay?" he asked me as he was stepping toward the door.

"I am just fine," I said in reply, ushering for him to go out the door.

"Wonderful! Thank you! I'm getting her back!" The oddball sprinted toward his muscle car and peeled out of the lot, not giving an ounce of care for the safety of the Californians he served on a daily basis who were driving and walking in his wake. He had even placed a siren on top of his car so he could rush toward his destination.

As I humorously watched him drive away, I returned to my seat, ready to gather my own items. As my purse began being filled with my keys and wallet, my eyebrows shot up in shock and frustration. "Motherfucker!"

"What?" my barista asked, her voice hoarse from laughter.

"He took my daisies!" I said, looking at my empty table and the petals that fell upon the floor.

She began laughing once again, and I walked out of the shop with a freshly brewed cup of heaven. I was more than happy to return to my life of routine. Even though I didn't end up with the green-eyed stranger, at least I was only caught in his riptide of confusion for a single encounter.

IV: Confessions of a Catholic Woman

I am a strong, proud Catholic woman
I also love the comforts of man
Yet I am unmarried, unclaimed in the eyes of God

My actions are of a sinner, my desires of a sinner, my needs of a sinner
It didn't bother me before
The hunger
The urge
The way my palms sweat and my saliva would collect on the underside of my tongue when a man of pure beauty and mystery would enter my presence.
Almost if fangs would drop from my canines and my eyes would burst from their amber confines into lust riddled emerald

He used to like my eyes
The way they would look at him

I am a strong proud Catholic woman
I have been taught in the ways of the Lord to have more self control
To practice patience and to pray for peace in my soul

If only that peace would calm the fire within my core which radiates like the sun

People look to me now for an example of a faith driven life
I know my prayers
I am confident in my relationship with God
I have nothing to hide if you asked
Yet there is a creature inside me always hungry, always lusting, always wanting him
It doesn't matter who he is

I am a strong proud Catholic woman
I know I can find comfort in confession
Share my desires with a priest to be my own tether to God
Ask for my penance and put my desires away
Yes, that is what I shall do
Then why does it feel like I am entering a jail cell, and not the safety of a confessional?
Why is my heart racing as I prepare the words of my confession?
I know what I have done, I feel no shame
Yet as I step closer to the doors, my knees begin to shake
Is this pride, oh Lord? Is this agony? Is this fear?
Why is this sacrament crushing me so?

It is my turn
My Confession, my Acceptance, My Truth
Surrounded by angels cloaked in shelter unseen by the mortal eye, I am taken into the room
It smells of incense and regret
I cannot see him, thank God
Yet everyone in this small town knows who I am
Oh God, my throat is closing
Can I do this? Will I do this?

Forgive me Father, for I have sinned

It has been… a while… since my last confession
Go on, he tells me
An invitation to continue
From there the angels unlock the chains trapping my voice in a box of denial
My truth pours out into a pond of wine, honesty coloring the grapes with tones of burgundy and pain

I am a strong proud Catholic woman
I love the comforts of sex outside of marriage
However, I am so incredibly alone
How can that be, Oh God? How can I be so alone?

My words leave my voice raspy, as if I spoke in front of thousands, yet it is only God and this kind priest that hear my pain
I am prepared for the judgment, for the condemnation, for the ridicule

Instead, he tells me the Lord loves me
Instead, he tells me I am not a deviant, a monster, a liar
No, instead, I am a woman and that my partner is close by

How can this be? How am I not punished? How can I receive this blessing when I have done so much wrong?
My loneliness is my punishment, my loneliness is the sign, my loneliness is God's cry for me to change and prepare myself for that partner waiting for me in life
My penance is to say three Hail Mary's and to ask for the Lord's eyes to see myself as he does.

My time is over
I must leave the confessional
While my heart is leaping with relief, my legs are weighted with lead
How can this truly be?

I kneel before him and I pray
The rising Christ only looks to me with love and compassion
How have I been so wrong for so long?

I am a strong proud Catholic woman
I have been humbled, I have been forgiven, I have been loved
In order for me to love him, to love my partner in life
I must love myself

V: Destiny Is to Be Determined

My soul mate died in the Twin Towers attacks of September 11, 2001.

At least that is what I would tell myself.

I was in the shower, Pantene Pro-V shampoo lathered in my hair, while my pink-and-gray shower radio played tunes from the 98.1 KJUG country-music radio station. I always enjoyed waking up an hour before my two sisters. They would hog up so much of the bathroom time and often make us late since our mom had to drive us to different campuses. I would take the extra hour for some added shower-karaoke time. I would allow myself to believe that I was the next Faith Hill or Trisha Yearwood. Occasionally, my mom would yell through the wall to silence my poor vocal ability. However, I would just keep smiling and sing along with the next song with progressively louder volume.

That morning, Lee Greenwood's "God Bless the USA" began playing over the pink-and-gray radio. I didn't know all the words, but I hummed along as I scrubbed myself down with a loofah full of Olay body wash. When the song ended, the ordinarily enthusiastic radio announcer came on with a somber tone. He could barely communicate the horrific knowledge that terrorism had come to American soil. I heard my mother scream, and I rushed out of the shower with plenty of soap suds in my hair.

I entered her dark-lavender bedroom, which she affectionately called her cave. My mother suffered from intense chronic migraines and needed deep darkness to combat the paralyzing pain that Excedrin and Diet Coke couldn't fix. The light from the news channel on her television felt so glaring to my early-morning eyes, yet as the screen turned shades of gray, black, and orange, the darkening tones did not ease my spirit. Instead, with caution and disbelief, I took a timid seat next to my mother, her silent tears falling like waterfalls of compassion and empathy down her cheeks.

There was so much to process on that traumatic day. Parents were invited to stay at schools the whole day so that they could be near their children. The universal feeling of devastation and assault struck every person in different ways. My youngest sister began developing unexplained spots all over her body. Discussions of the attacks paired with the fact that our father worked for a nuclear-power plant practicing terrorism-simulation drills gave the doctors enough evidence to assume that her spots were brought on by stress and anxiety. September 11 would become my emotional crutch much later in life.

As the years passed, my experiences with men would be a continuous roller coaster of events. Some would be kind, some would be funny, and others would be downright rude and hateful. Yet through all my encounters, finding the right man just couldn't happen for me. I almost made it a game. If I could get a second date, I'd earn a Tootsie Pop. Sounds crazy, but my track record wasn't the best.

On the ten-year anniversary of the September 11 attacks, I was making dinner for my grandparents and enjoying some needed zinfandel wine. We laughed in the living room and discussed the day-to-day ins and outs of our lives. When it came time for coffee after dinner, Grampa suggested us moving to the entertainment room and enjoying some television. When the anniversary special came on, our jovial tone turned into one of reverence. The footage of crumbling buildings, decimated bodies, and heartbroken loved ones left us all quiet and brokenhearted for our fellow citizens.

On the lower quarter of the television was a list of names being cycled through. The thousands that died ten years ago were being remembered and acknowledged. While we watched a story about a family who lost their father in the attacks, a flame of awareness burned within me. Maybe I wasn't alone because of my own choices or the fact that the men I dated just weren't right for me. Maybe I was alone because my soul mate died that day. We never had a chance to fall in love or to be together because it was stolen in a heap of airplane fuel and tragedy.

In my silence, my emotion-filled and hormone-charged brain began breaking down the mathematical possibilities of my theory. I had a tendency to date older men, which allowed my dating range to be quite large. I took into account the percentage of single straight men who were in the buildings and planes and weighed the probability that they were at the location of the attacks by mistake and that their loss would impact both our spiritual and metaphysical timelines. His loss from life robbed us of happiness and companionship. Yes, this was the solution I had sought.

With a long drink from my wine glass and the wiping away of fresh tears, my mind began reconciling my theory about my current state of severe longing with the loss of so many lives on September 11. For years, the soul mate–interruptus theory governed my subconscious. Romantic failures and rejections became easier and easier to accept due to the fact that those I engaged with were never my true partner in the first place. He was brutally taken from me before I ever knew him. His spirit was just as lonely as I was, whether it be in heaven, another dimension, or a rebirthed life. My chronic loneliness became easier to digest as I believed that my partner was just as incomplete elsewhere.

It took many years and a liquid confession for the soul mate–interruptus theory to be shared aloud. My dearest friend, one with the most beauty and charisma that I've ever known, was navigating her way through her first true heartbreak. He wasn't her first or last lover; however, he was the only one up to this time in our life who made her contemplate marriage and forever. He challenged her with heated debates and lubricated her with vodka and coconut oil as they tumbled their way through a flash of love and passion. They hurt each other often with drunken, careless words, yet their love for each other couldn't be denied.

It was during an evening of true friendship that my own theory stumbled out of my mouth and into reality. It was a burning Fourth of July, yet broken pieces of my beautiful friend's heart were what I was gathering in my hands instead of sparklers. As she rested her head against my body, shaking from another disappointing and devastating encounter with her lover, I held on to her tightly on my couch, staying silent and offering pieces of encouragement as she wept. With some spirited whiskey, we began our sharing of our frustrations with men and why they are oblivious to when they hurt us the most. Her blue eyes were captured by a cloak of salty red tears, her black mascara dripping onto her cheeks and spreading across my shirt.

She made a comment about how she would never understand why she had to endure such pain. I replied with complete confidence, "That's why I'm glad my soul mate died on 9/11."

Her crying stopped, her shoulders tensed, and she stiffly turned her neck toward my face. "What?"

Shit! I thought to myself, realizing that my theory had been revealed. "Um . . . yes. Have you heard of soul mate interruptus?"

"No. That isn't a thing," she replied.

"Okay, I made it up." I sat back. "It's my belief—my theory, really—that each of us has a soul mate. Due to the circumstances of our lives, they come when it has been destined. However, my theory—hence soul mate interruptus—is that my soul mate was taken during the 9/11 attacks."

Taken away from her own thoughts about her previous heartbreak, she continued the investigation of my theory. "Why September 11, Rachel?"

"It makes the most mathematical sense. You know how much I love older men and how much I love men from the East Coast—"

"Oh my god!"

"Well, taking all the factors into account, narrowing down the single straight men who were the victims in the buildings and on the planes, it is possible that my soul mate died that day and that I am currently alone because he is alone in another metaphysical plane or dimension."

Silence greeted me. Her eyes were looking me up and down. I could feel my heart racing as I watched her conduct the math I just gave her into her mind. She took a moment to nod, and then she looked down at her teal sweatpants, her fingers playing with the tie strings on the ends by her calves.

What struck me with surprise was the new set of tears that coated her eyes when she looked back at me. She shook her head in disbelief, sadness coating her smile in a gloss of tears and Burt's Bees lip balm. "Oh, Rachel."

She crawled over to me and pulled me into her arms, her grip tight as her sobs escaped her. Startled, I held on to her and rubbed her back with my hands, hoping to calm her.

After a few moments, she looked up at me and wiped away her tears. "You have barricaded your heart behind a theory so lonely that you convinced yourself that your person is dead—not just broken up with but literally dead. Rach, you deserve everything. Your heart, your goodness—I promise you he is out there. He is out there, waiting for you. I'm so sorry that you have been in so much pain."

"But I'm not—"

"You are," she interrupted. "I promise you that when he does appear, your soul will know. Just like mine did. It will be okay. We will be okay."

I had no words to give her after she had her moment of clarity. I continued to console her through her heartbreak.

She had fallen asleep, and my Zuzu was in her arms as she began to escape into her broken dreams. As I sat at my kitchen table, finishing my own glass of whiskey, the rumbling of my heart sent my heart beating fiercely, my hands shaking, and my throat closing with burning tears. With my teeth clenched, I took a cautious sip to finish my drink. Alone with my thoughts, my best friend's words began deconstructing the theory that explained my loneliness for nearly ten years. I could barely breathe as the reality of my solitary existence began having no explanation that could be acceptable to my longing other than the fact that I was romantically and emotionally incompatible. *What am I even doing?*

With the greatest attempt for silence in fear of waking my friend, I allowed the dam to break and my tears to fall. The reality was that the soul mate–interruptus theory was a shield I created for myself to keep me from feeling desperate and broken in the absence of my significant other. With the shudders of my sobs, I could feel my hands burning, the ache for hands to hold them tight burning to the point of imagined redness upon my skin.

As I collected myself from the discovery of the probability that soul mate interruptus was not a solid theory, I began looking around my apartment and gauging everything that I loved and cared for before me. My sisters were sound asleep with my Tiger Lily, while Zuzu guarded my best friend against her heartbreak-riddled night terrors. The whiskey I consumed warmed my body, and I was blessed to be living in a city full of life and diversity.

Yes, I was currently without my soul mate. However, that didn't mean that it would be that way forever. Maybe it was time for me to take a step away from the soul mate–interruptus theory and learn to engage with men in a more hopeful and future-minded way. Maybe he was out there, waiting for me with similarly burning hands.

My soul's journey may already be on a destined path, yet there is room for more detours along the way.

VI: EVER PREPARED

Hello, thank you for meeting with me today.

My name is Rachel Kovach, and I am interviewing you to be my next romantic partner.

I apologize, have you not been on a date in 2018?

Allow me the privilege of walking you through these messy steps.

Watch out! There may be pieces of baggage that drop overhead.

It can knock into you and alter your path.

I am unsure how heavy the luggage is... good luck!

I doubt that we met in a classic meet cute format.

That would be just too adorable for these cynical times that we live in.

I believe you viewed one of my half dozen profiles that exist in the dating realm.

Is it my casually flirtatious profile on Tinder?

I am advertised as loving red wine and quiet nights indoors.

Is it my effervescent Bumble profile?

You must love walking my two three legged dogs before and after a mandatory coffee break.

Or is it my faulty Match.com profile?

I worked really hard to answer the dozens of free algorithm formulating questions that could present me to the hundreds of potential soul mates that live in a 50 mile radius of Los Angeles.

Are none of these the right option? Okay, let's move forward.

I really appreciate you taking the time out of your busy schedule to meet with me. Between hours of community service opportunities, coffee therapy sessions with friends and phone calls with my very involved family, it is trying to make time for myself.

I am really captivated by your eyes. Your eyes and your smile are what drew me into swiping right and hoping we'd be a match.

Now I know that you must be somewhat intelligent. I don't meet up with anyone that leaves me messages on my profile that aren't grammatically correct.

Thank you for not sending me a needless photo of your genitals. It is an immediate turnoff.
I am unsure why men believe our mouths water at the sight of a strategically positioned penis.
Women mastered the art of perfecting flattering camera angles before men decided to bring it down below and show off their favorite feature.
It is quite disappointing to expect Paul Bunyan and meet Mighty Mouse.

So tell me a little bit about yourself.
What do you like?
What is your profession?
What is your passion?

My heart is racing.

You've reached out to hold my hand and look directly into my eyes as you share your many global adventures.

While I am sitting, I can feel my knees begin to shake.

So far it's going well. Well enough that I need to reapply my lipstick.

I don't trust you enough to leave my drink behind.

However, the bartender made quite a strong Old Fashioned.

I can walk away and leave you to your smartphone and quiet conversational skills until I return.

Or it may be enough time to drug my drink.

Okay, uncertainty is winning in this heartbeat of a moment.

I must chug this drink with urgency before using the restroom.

Don't be alarmed, I don't have a drinking problem.

I have a trusting problem.

You smile gently as I excuse myself to use the restroom, good job.

I took my purse with me to review my essentials:

Lipstick, check.

Condoms, check.

Cash, check.

Phone on silent, check.

I'm adjusting my appearance,

Lifting the breasts ever so slightly,

Assessing my dress to be sure it isn't showing off the wrong curves...

Okay, I'm ready for the second part of this intervi-- date.

Oh no.

You ruined it.

You're on a dating app while we are on a date...

Really?

I wasn't gone more than five minutes.

Were you so impatient that you had to look at your options while I was away?
Or have you been charming me with your fantastic looks and aura of confidence to hide the fact that you don't see us being compatible for more than just this evening?

Ugh, I feel gross.

I can tell you noticed my knowing glance upon your screen as I returned to my seat.
Your posture becomes more distant.
Our hands are no longer joined.

We are simply two strangers sitting in a common dining area.
We couldn't be further apart.

I ask for the check when our waiter passes by.
You ask me what is wrong.
I tell you I might have caught a bug at work.

Your compassion is quite endearing.
If I hadn't seen other women on your screen, I may be inclined to invite you home with me.

Instead I am building protective measures around my heart,
My mind is made up.
This is going no further.

I thank you for taking the time, once again, to meet with me.

As you navigate your next romantic exploration, I hope you value being present.

Value one another.

Appreciate the time they have taken to meet with you.

Don't be so quick to launch to the next best thing.

You never know what you'll be walking away from,

Or what tornado of baggage lies ahead.

VII: FLIRTATION AND FEAR—A DOUBLE-EDGED SWORD

Have you ever been so comfortable with comfortable that you allow perfectly wonderful opportunities to slip away? Yep, that is me in a nutshell. I am indeed a fearful flirt.

I wasn't always this way. I can remember being young and bold, sitting in men's laps in my toddler years, turning their heads, and saying, "Pay attention to me!" What was once so endearing and adorable to adults feels like a shadow of me. The woman I am now can barely contain her devastating need to control her environment and how people, particularly men, perceive her.

Being a woman of the modern era, I am independent and strong. Much like Diana of *Wonder Woman*, I believe in truth and justice. I believe that a woman can do anything a man can do and, when given the opportunity, can often do it better. And yet, the warrior in me dies a little each time I find myself ignored or disregarded by the object of my affections. I am a better runner than a confrontationalist in the realm of romance.

I chuckle as I think of the flirtation and fear inside of me, which take the forms of my two three-legged Jindo dogs, Tiger Lily and Zuzu. Both of my girls are survivors of the meat trade in Korea, where they were victims of a form of human cruelty that can make most vomit.

Tiger Lily, the eldest of the two sisters, endured the most torture in the meat markets. She lived in captivity, her front arm taken piece by piece for human consumption, and she was forced to produce a litter of puppies but not allowed to mother them. She watched her babies be taken away from her after their birth. While so much of what my eldest girl went through is horrific, I believe that crime against animalkind was what broke her heart the most.

I rescued my Tiger Lily just over a month after my Charlie, a beagle of the most regal and loving nature, died tragically and suddenly of a burst spinal disc. Tiger Lily was known as Ho Soon at the animal-rescue organization by the name of Tails of the Wind, which is in Sun Valley, California. I had no intention of adopting another dog so quickly after my Charlie's passing. However, after a caring nudge from my father, I knew that it was time to start putting a balm on the festering wound within my heart that wouldn't stop bleeding.

Tiger Lily was wild and fearful. Her brindle fur shined in the light as she blended so well into her environment. Her thin frame shook as she ran in helpless circles. She reminded me of horses that are trained out of their wild spirit. Her honey-brown eyes held so much pain. I remember asking the owner of the shelter if it was safe to approach her. With a heartbroken smile, she shared that Tiger Lily was the only dog she had ever rescued that did not attempt to bite her when she opened her cage for the first time. Instead, she shrunk away in fear of what mankind might do to her. My own heart broke a little more as I stared at the tortured creature, her anxiety radiating off her in exhausting waves.

As I knelt in the dirt where she was running, I leaned against a wooden column. She wasn't able to get closer than six feet from me before her breathing rate increased and her anxiety spiked. I sat in relative silence for just over an hour before I turned and saw her crawl closer to me—not by much, just closer. I took that moment to study her more carefully, getting angrier at the evidence of the cruelties humanity could do to such innocent animals in the name of making an extra dollar. Gently I brought my hand forward, and I was able to touch her head softly. Her tall ears were remarkably soft—a dash of innocence among her lifetime of suffering. With a tearful smile, I asked if she was willing to help me heal if I could help her heal at the same time. With a subtle stillness, she leaned ever so slightly into my hand—a cautious acceptance of our new life together.

While Tiger has grown tremendously in the years I have loved her, she is still governed by fear and traumatic reaction. I often find myself filled with feelings of jealousy and outrage when I witness her give her affections to men and strangers, yet when I call her name, she skittishly trots around the park in a Forrest Gump–style fashion. Tiger Lily is often the spirit that roams my own heart when I find that men are getting too close to me. I take timid steps forward, ready to make a move, my opportunity for feelings of love and passion just millimeters away from me. Yet when he turns around and confronts me with feelings of anger, disgust, or worse, compliance, the wild spirit of Tiger Lily roars, and I find myself charging toward the furthest corner that my heart can find so that he can't see that he was that close to me.

My wild Tiger Lily fears may be one half of my soul, yet the fiery, passionate, and flirtatious part of me is embodied in my youngest dog, Zuzu. A fighter from the moment she was born in a Korean slaughterhouse, Zuzu had her leg caught in a trap, and she pulled herself out of the slaughterhouse and her impending death into the streets of her village. It is with great fortune that Zuzu was collected immediately by the rescue organization that saved my Tiger Lily just ten months prior. They had intended on raising her to perfect health before putting her up for adoption on the global sector. However, the slaughterhouse had found the rescue and demanded their property be returned to them. With much sarcasm, the organization sent the trap Zuzu's leg had been claimed in as their response. Before authorities could be involved, the organization sent a message to all the previous adopters, including myself, to see if they could get Zuzu out of the country. The moment I saw her small puppy face and the ridiculously endearing stump upon her back leg, I knew she was my girl. I accepted the role of rescuing Zuzu and made arrangements for her to be sent to Los Angeles.

When I arrived at Los Angeles Airport's Tom Bradley Terminal, I was impressed to be greeted with the Korean correspondent of the organization that was based in California. With hugs and happiness, we eagerly awaited the arrival of Zuzu with her human carrier. It was during the moments of waiting that it was brought to my attention that Zuzu's papers needed to be fudged a little bit in order for her to come to the United States. Surprised, I asked which area had to be altered. The correspondent shared that it was Zuzu's age that needed to be adjusted. According to international trade laws, animals cannot be transported if they are younger than six months of age. I then asked how old this puppy was and was surprised to find that she was only two and a half months old.

Three hours later, my shock had lessened as the carrier made her way through the airport, my new addition sleeping in her carrier. We met her outside of the airport, my hands shaking with excitement.

"Be careful," the correspondent warned me. "Many experience feelings of intense love and belonging when they open their carriers. It feels like destiny."

After nodding, I turned my eyes toward the closing mechanism of the door, pressed it together, and released a sigh of relief as I pulled open the metal door. My eyes were immediately drawn to the ball of white fluff, and then I saw the chocolate-brown eyes of the infant pup. With a small yawn, she stood with excitement and carefully walked toward my eager hands. Trembling, I held her torso and brought her into my arms. Much like the Grinch when he felt the meaning of Christmas, I felt my heart grow three times its size, and this infant pup's kisses filled my spirit with more joy than it had in months. This small tripod created her own space in my heart and world from the moment she met my eyes.

As I raised Zuzu with Tiger Lily, her vibrant personality evolved in daily waves of entertainment. There was no petal or leaf on the ground that she didn't speak to. Her speed did not slow with the lack of her hind leg. Zuzu's love for men was the talk of our neighborhood park as she demanded their attention with barks and cuddles. She asserted her dominance over younger pups with strong stances and warning growls. Yet with the corrective call of her name, Zuzu rolls on the ground in submission, seeking validation and forgiveness.

Zuzu's brazen personality mirrors my own as I make myself known to the men I encounter. I allow commanding flirtation and batting eyelashes to set the tone for romance. While I don't like correction, I turn heads with a single heavy sigh or disgruntled pout.

Flirtation and fear, Tiger Lily and Zuzu, the two halves of me that dictate much of my dating persona. It is a daunting task to pursue another person and control the wolves of control within ourselves that tell us to fight or flee. My wolves happen to be three-legged Jindos who have taught me more about how to be brave than I could have ever expected.

VIII: Generosity: Giving versus Receiving

Glancing across the smoky bar
I can't help but wonder who you are.
No shining star or hidden wish
Could have prepared me for what I stumbled upon.

Reaching for your clear and mischievous drink,
My mouth waters as you lick the salt off the rim of the glass
Green eyes with flecks of gold invite me
My knees tremble and beg to kneel before your male beauty.

Instinctively, I move away
Prepare myself for another lover
Too short, too odd, no compatibility for me
Why do I feel a burning sensation in the back of my head?

Enjoying the view, I take a moment
To truly assess the mysterious man before me
Tall and brooding is very much my style,
Your leather belt is begging me to remove it with my teeth.

Voluptuous is what I am,
My curves work hard to define me.
The pawing hands and nibbles from strangers
Remind me of my sensual power.

Consequently, your eyes begin to explore my form
Your teeth biting your lower lip with anticipation
With a sultry wink and a flip of my hair
I believe I have won this round.

In foolishness was that assumption
Your form coming quickly behind me
Your heat, your power, your purpose
Send my head back to find a home in your chest.

Enjoying your victory in our battle,
Your hands come upon my wanton hips
As we sway to the pulsing beat
Or is it the musky heat?

Needing more of you, I turn my body to toward your face
Your beard roughly marring my rosy cheek
With a groan, I thrust forward,
My lips upon your collar bone

Violently, you take my lips as your own
My arms wrapped around your neck to stay steady
Our tongues fighting for dominance
Our souls lost in the haze

Gasping for air, my grip tight in your hair
Yours equally tugging my blonde mane
A silent agreement, a nod in the night
We need to get out of here immediately

Enchanting Sensuality, Giving versus Receiving
Generosity a wicked web of push and pull
No shining star or hidden wish
Could have prepared us for what we stumbled upon.

IX: HEART ATTACK
(RK ARTS)

X: Instaloving or Instalosing?

In 1995, Gary Kremen and Peng T. Ong launched Match.com, the world's first online-dating website, after building a successful relationship-matchmaking business in 1993. Oh, how I loathe and appreciate these modern yentas. Utilizing mathematical algorithms and a culture of loneliness, Kremen and Ong worked to help the overscheduled find love, companionship, and long-term relationships through the completion of dozens of questions, geographical points of origin, and the enlistment of the financial support of thousands of previously broken hearts. It helped so many that other entrepreneurs decided to invest in the endless vat of broken hearts and create love connections one membership at a time.

Launching forward in time into the 2010s, anyone with a smartphone has quickly realized that their time and attention are based heavily on their smartphones and their cyber conversations. Instant gratification has become the norm. People no longer need to bump into someone at their local dive bar or coffee shop to find love when they have dozens of applications that they can swipe left and right with their finger to determine their interest. Dating websites have blossomed and have become individualized to meet the needs of dozens of subgroups. From the dog lovers to the military spouses, from the partygoers to the book lovers, there has been a dating application developed for every kind of person. Yet the world, for all its technological connections, still feels so lonely, so distant, and so aggressive.

In my twenty-third year of life, I caved and decided to expand from free dating applications to an actual dating subscription. Through eharmony's dating interface, I answered over five hundred questions in the first two weeks in hopes that it would guide me to my fellow broken hearts in the cyber universe. Some of the questions included were the following:

Do you want kids?
Do you drink?
If you were a fruit, what fruit would you be and why?
Do you think you are a good listener?
Can there be one soul mate for every person?
Is religion a big deal?
Do you enjoy holidays?
Do you like your family?
Would you consider kissing another person on the mouth cheating?
Would you smoke a cigarette from a homeless person?

All the questions seemed to swirl into a protein shake of despair as I completed them in the sanctuary of my bedroom with a glass of wine and my lessened dignity. Going to bed, I told myself I would try this cyber-dating adventure for six months. If nothing would pan out, I'd cancel and eat the $159.99 cost with my pride intact. Oh, how wrong I was by that prediction.

As a teacher, it is very difficult to date online. When people see your profession, you tend to get two different responses from potential suitors: First, you have the people that have now placed you on a shelf of sainthood; you are now unattainable, and they are unwilling to shift you away from a perspective of eternal compassion and empathy. The average introductory comments include "Oh, your job must be so fulfilling!" and "You are doing the Lord's work!" and "I could never work with kids! How you can handle being around all those children all day is beyond me!" The second round of comments is much more sexual in nature. Some of these comments include "Oh, are you a good teacher or a naughty teacher?" "What would you do to me in detention?" and my personal favorite, "Do you have rulers at home that you can spank me with?" After a couple months of sifting through the crap, labeling my profession from teacher to working in the field of education was a way to solve some of those problems.

Getting eharmony alerts on my phone while teaching was a challenge as well. Some don't seem to realize that I can't chat during school days. While I was breaking down the distributive property to a room full of teenagers, my phone was receiving sexually energized messages that hoped for scheduled dates and casual sex. From balancing grades to cute guys, eharmony didn't seem like a match for me.

That was until the farmer.

It was a brisk autumn day. Students were surviving midterms with block schedules. Those block schedules let me work with my primary teacher, make copies, collaborate with other assistants, and organize my own life from my safe desk. Taking a moment to breathe away from the wave of questions pertaining to government, economics, and history, I looked down at my phone and started to complete my social-media rounds.

As I was exploring the chaotic world of Facebook, I received an alert that said I found a new match on eharmony. When I opened the application, I was greeted with the following question:

"Do you believe there is life outside of earth?"

Surprised that I hadn't answered the question previously, I responded to my new gentleman friend with the following answer:

"It would be ignorant of me to believe that we are the only life existing in the universe. So yes, I do believe there is life outside of earth. Have a nice day."

Satisfied with my response, I slipped my phone back into my desk and returned to work with no intention of going back to my device until the end of the day. That was until I heard the buzzing.

He wrote back so quickly! After making sure that I was still alone, I opened his message, which said,

---

"Oh, I am so relieved to hear you say that! We are damaging our earth every day. It is so important for us to start making connections with other life forms outside of Earth. They will be our refuge when we receive word that we must evacuate our native planet. Also, do you like chicken wings?"

Oh god, I thought to myself. *He is either an insane environmentalist or a crazed space enthusiast.* Suddenly, his voice began sounding like Buzz Lightyear's.

Great, another dud. Okay then. Better to know now rather than later, I told myself. Taking my phone with me to the restroom, I gave myself enough time to construct a fair and honest objection to my newest match that could leave us wishing each other the best in their future dating endeavors.

"Thank you so much for reaching out. Yes, I do enjoy chicken wings; however, I do believe that you and I want different things. I wish you the best as you find your match in love."

There—it's over. God, three more months until I can deactivate this thing. While shaking my head, I sent the response, and then I returned to my classroom. As I walked, my phone vibrated with urgency. In bold letters, he replied to my rejection with words that stopped me in my tracks.

"No! Wait! I need you to fulfill my blonde quota!"

Suddenly, I was overcome with curiosity and disgust—disgust that such a man would have quotas for women but curious as to what he could mean by such a comment.

"Excuse me?"

I walked into my dear friend's English classroom, her room organized in a way that allowed students to begin exploring Macbeth while remembering that they were indeed sitting in a Southern California classroom. When she saw me shaking my head, she immediately started laughing; she wanted to know what she assumed was my latest student- or staff-related problem.

"Girl, I can't even with dating anymore."

"What happened?" she asked.

"So I'm on eharmony—don't judge! And I got a message from a farmer asking if I believed there was life outside of earth."

"Sexy," she responded with a sarcastic smirk.

"I know! Ugh. After telling him I wasn't interested, he said that he needed me to fulfill his blonde quota!"

"Ew! Wait, what?!" Her vibrant blue eyes were filled with confusion and hysterical concern as I shook my head in disbelief.

With a laugh, I shoved my now-buzzing phone toward her. "He wrote back! He wrote back! Tell me what he said!"

"Okay!" she said with a laugh.

After opening my iPhone 5C, she started by screaming, and then she sat in her reclining leather computer chair and laughed hysterically. "Oh, Rach . . ."

"Tell me! Tell me!"

After taking a breath to control her laughter, she read his response aloud:

"You see, this planet is going to die in the next eighteen months. I have a redhead and brunette ready to repopulate the human race with me on the International Space Station. Now I just need a blonde. You, with your blonde hair and career interest in education, can not only fulfill the quota but also educate our children as they learn about humanity before we inhabited space."

By the time she finished the message, my ribs were screaming in agony. I continued to laugh at my love life's misfortune. Shaking my head, I said, "What do I do with that?!"

"Nothing! Absolutely nothing!" she replied. "Actually, maybe frame it and remember this forever."

"Oh god," I groaned. I took the phone back and walked toward the doors.

"You didn't see the crop circles when you matched?" she asked.

"Crop circles?" I asked.

"Look at his profile picture."

While studying his photo, I started to see the errors in my initial screening of my newest match. Yes, he did wear overalls and a cap, which led to the quick assumption that he was a farmer. However, the jean jacket with the NASA emblem and the crop circles in the background proved that he wasn't Old McDonald.

"I thought he was a farmer."

"No, he definitely belongs to the world beyond. Phone home, Rach! Phone home!"

While walking back to my classroom, I wiped away my tears of laughter and embarrassment and returned to my tasks. Taking one more look at my entertaining phone, I went to eharmony and blocked my space enthusiast. While it may seem conservative to some, exploring a love beyond Earth isn't what I am looking for.

XI: Junk in the Trash (RK Arts)

XII: Knowing They Are "the One"

After nineteen months of disasters, I had found him. I had found my match. Yes, it had included subscribing to yet another online community with my credit card information, but I knew this was it. From the profile pictures he chose, I could tell he was a single dad who enjoyed fishing and trucks. His blue eyes appeared kind, and his height and smile made my heart skip a beat. This was the chance at love that I'd been waiting for.

Who can go wrong with a dating site that is founded on discovering single and available military personnel to be your romantic match? These brave soldiers have sacrificed so much for our safety and the safety of our allies. They have walked away from normalcy to defend each citizen that survives in this roller coaster of a nation. It was the least I could do to provide their matchmakers my quickly expiring sixteen-digit plastic identity with the leap of faith that I could be a soul mate that could serve as a passionate anchor here at home.

His name is . . . well, from what I could gather, his name is MDxn4888. When I was young, I always thought my soul mate would be very much like Dean Cain in his portrayal of Clark Kent and Superman. However, MDxn4888 took a step toward a mysterious direction. I've known many men whose names begin with *M*—Matthew, Mark, Malyik, Morrison, etc. I'd just need to be patient and be ready for when I met him.

We set our location. Based on his profile, I assumed he liked sports bars. He suggested a location and time in our chat box. I set my phone timer for three minutes to appear that I was looking at my overbooked schedule, and then I confirmed the time. After a quick Google search, I found that this establishment appeared to be on the casual side. Again, while referencing his profile, I found that we both held on to a desperate loyalty to the San Francisco 49ers. So my aged Joe Montana jersey and tight black jeans and heels would have to do.

As a woman, I have found it is important for me to arrive just a bit earlier than my date in order to grab a drink and spot on the bar as well as mentally plan exit strategies if the date turns to crap. However, that wasn't going to happen this time. MDxn4888 was going to be the match. I wouldn't need an exit plan because we would be leaving together. Yep, I believed this was going to work. I arrived fifteen minutes early though just as a precaution.

I entered the smoky bar, the aged burn of Marlboros encompassing me in a cloud of impending desperation. The clinking of my red heels drew the attention of many men at the bar who had been previously focused on the hockey game playing above the full bar. I smiled gently, leaned against the bar, ordered an old-fashioned, and took a moment to mentally identify the exits.

"An old-fashioned? Damn, woman. You go fast!" I heard from behind me.

Turning my head, I was prepared to be greeted with blue eyes. Instead, I found green eyes with specks of amber within them. His dark hair was shaggy and fell below his ears. Wearing a tight gray T-shirt, this man leaned against the bar, his eyes appraising me much like a person would while selecting a used car in a dealership. His smile was full of confidence and swagger, his need to succeed in this flirtation radiating off him desperately like the Axe cologne he had chosen to wear.

Not intending to be rude but having no interest in pursuing the conversation, I nodded and then grabbed my drink from the barman. Taking a step aside, I spotted a corner table with plenty of visual-access points. I took a seat and looked down at my phone.

I was officially on time for our date. *Where are you, MDxn4888?* I thought to myself.

Thirty minutes passed, and the precipitation began falling against the crystal, which began heightening my anxiety. I took a sip of the amber liquid to calm my nerves and to begin mentally deducting dating points from my tardy companion. Turning on my phone, I used the camera app to double-check my makeup and make sure there wasn't a flaw in place. My mane of wavy blonde hair was down the correct part line. My vibrant purple eyeliner added a dash of personality to my amber eyes, so he wouldn't notice that they were shaped in two completely different ways—one almond-shaped and the other round. My Minnie Mouse bow–like lips were my favorite feature. Wrapped in a blanket of wine red, I knew that MDxn4888 wouldn't be able to stop from keeping his gaze upon them.

The cheers from the bar brought me out of my mental checklist. When I lifted my eyes, an ice bath of reality drowned me fiercely. Focusing my gaze at the pool table, my eyes were greeted by the sight of my date teaching another woman how to play pool. She was bent over the table, her vixen eyes playing up their doe-like characteristics as he wrapped his arms around her body to show her how to use the stick correctly. He took a drag from his beer and then leaned in to whisper in her ear, her eyes sparkling because of the innuendo-filled comment he gave her. She turned beneath him and hoisted her body onto the wooden edge in order to look up into his mischievous blue eyes. He took his moment, leaned down, and kissed her, his grip on her waist tightening as their encounter became more intense. She moved her long brown hair to the side as his lips made their way to claim her long neck.

My phone alarm went off, removing me quickly from my focused gaze. The alarm I had ironically set on my phone read, "Pretend your sister is sick and you need to leave." *There won't be a need for this alarm tonight,* I thought to myself. I got duped. Finishing my old-fashioned in a single gulp, I moved my hair to the side, smiled, and left the smoky corner.

As I walked past the bar, my teenage-smelling companion from earlier in the night lifted his glass toward me in a cheering fashion. After nodding to him, I went toward the exit doors. However, my need for male validation and injured pride took over my instincts. After pivoting, I went to the shaggy-haired man, turned him toward me, and pulled his face toward mine for a kiss. It was hard and demanding as I reclaimed my attractiveness. After fifteen seconds, I stepped away, and his green eyes were wider than I expected. He simply stared at me; his mouth dropped open while my wine-red lipstick stained his own. Winking, I whispered, "You're welcome," and then I went out the door. The bouncer gave me a high five as I exited the building and made my way toward my car.

Maybe MDxn4888 wasn't my Dean Cain. Maybe the vixen brunette was his Lois Lane and I happened to be part of the circumstance in which they met. I could have been the fortunate chess piece needed for them to begin their game of falling in love. I could have been completely wrong, and the shaggy-haired man could have been my true soul mate. Maybe I needed to look past the teenager trapped in a grown man's body and walk back into the bar so I could bring this brown-haired stranger home with me.

My smoky friend exited the bar. His torso rocked as if it was being thrown around by a tequila-driven roller coaster. His pale face turned a shade of yellow green that oddly complimented his eyes as he vomited outside the bar. "Damn, man!" the friendly bouncer said in disgust as my companion continued throwing up the liquid contents provided by the establishment.

Nope, I thought to myself, shaking my head at the moment of lapsed judgment. I turned on my car and drove away, alone and oddly content. The sound of Jason Aldean and Kelly Clarkson's duet, "Don't You Wanna Stay?" came over the radio, their pained love for each other nursing my rejection from earlier in the evening. *Dean Cain is out there,* I thought to myself. *When I find him, he'll ask me to stay—and hopefully not vomit on the sidewalk.*

XIII: Losing the Fantasy

I wish I was a vampire,
A werewolf, a shape shifter,
Another being not belonging to humanity.
If I was, it could explain these primal feelings inside of me.

Growing up, I fell into the dream of the fairy tale,
Seeking the joys of finding
The Prince Charming to my Cinderella,
The Prince Eric to my Ariel,
The Prince to Snow White, the fairest of them all,
I wanted to be swept off my feet, worshiped for my beauty and
taken away toward the sunset for my happily ever after.

However, my needs have become much baser, more hungry
Much like the supernaturals,
My wants not governed by man, but something greater,
With a darker purpose

No one tells you that you'll eventually want to stumble upon
Tarzan,
Allow his beastly instincts to take over,
Have him pound into you repeatedly,
Indoors, outdoors, from behind, blindfolded, tied up,

Your own grunts and cries getting lost in the jungle of your messy
bedroom.

No one tells you that you would trade Prince Charming in anyday
To be wrecked by a mountain of man
Whose erection is so mighty
You are tempted to faint in anticipation of your own release.

No, the fairy tales keep it much cleaner, much simpler.

When did my dreams shift away from the innocent story book
love
To such heated exchanges of bite marks and lipstick stains?
When did love songs become lullabies sung to children
And words of hot immediate need become my norm for the
invitation for temporary intimacy?

I wondered that the other night,
When I laid in his arms,
Not for long, for I don't cling to him too tightly,
I can't let him know I want to stay.

The sex was as thrilling as it usually is,
The feel of his forearms beneath my fingers is my weakness,
His bite marks on the underside of my breasts his own way of
claiming me.

He has mentioned that the idea of claiming me is an impossibility.

As I lay in our shared haze post encounter,
I took a moment to daydream, extending my stay just a little
longer…

What if claiming me wasn't impossible,
What if he decided to break down my walls and capture my
heart?

What if we stumbled through the lust filled haze into our own happily ever after?

I suddenly pictured his honey brown eyes looking me up and down with pride,
Our little ones chasing sea shells along the shore,
My left hand rubbing my expanding stomach with another of our creations inside it,
He lets go of my hand to chase our children down the glistening sand,
As he lets me go --

He releases me in his arms and turns over,
A satisfied snore escaping his mouth,
His head nuzzling into his pillow just as he had just done moments ago within my cleavage.

No, he won't come after me,
For I have made it impossible,
The fantasy is gone, no longer a possibility.
Why have these tears dropped from my eyes?

Rolling out of bed, I return my clothes to my naked form,
Quietly I leave the lust filled fantasy,
Wondering if love and hunger could ever truly coexist.

XIV: Marriage and Its Consequences

Our encounter was not meant to be beautiful.

On the contrary, it was heated, quick, and we didn't take off all our clothes.

He was unhappy. I was broken by my own series of heartbreaks and losses that were completely unrelated to romance.

So we stumbled onto this moment. We met at a party for our mutual friends who were celebrating their buying their first home. I hadn't even noticed him at first. I was so focused on cheering on my friend's newest accomplishment and navigating my way to the wine table as quickly as possible.

I had heard arguing from the backyard. I saw him getting yelled at by a woman who was about my height and who held a fierce position of control and authority. While he was incredibly tall, he seemed so small in stature—a frail scarecrow hanging in the cornfield of Los Angeles. He nodded, his eyes seemingly checked out from her tirade. He lifted his gaze and found my eyes. Smiling sadly, I lifted my drink toward him, wishing him luck as he continued to be publicly assassinated. His female companion looked deflated as she finished her series of complaints. She left him standing in the backyard, clearly confused by her newest tantrum.

I could feel a burning from behind my neck, yet the weather outside was crisp with autumn air. With each step around the apartment, the heat was intensifying. Glancing left and glancing right, I could not find what was piercing me so, setting my body on fire.

I was walking around the gaggle of couples who were chatting against the fireplace when I felt his hand grip my forearm. The burning returned. His brown eyes looked lonely. I knew the feeling all too well. Wordlessly I followed him up the stairs.

We were in their guest restroom; it was not quite as small as an airplane stall, yet it left our bodies pressed against each other. His fractured onyx eyes were filled with hurt and frustration. It was as if his death grip on my arm mirrored the hurricane of emotions within my own soul.

He opened his mouth to speak. I shook my head, not wanting to know. I brought his head down to mine and kissed him urgently. He hoisted me onto the bathroom sink, my dress riding up my thighs as he ground his body into mine. He was desperate to feel every inch of me as quickly as possible. I brought my lips down upon his collarbone as my hands made their way to his belt buckle. As my hand made contact with his aching member, he let loose a growl of need and hunger. I silenced him with my lips and continued pumping him up and down as he tried to control his urges. I knew he wouldn't last long, so I shifted my underwear to the side. He grabbed a condom from the bathroom cabinet. I was fortunate that my head didn't crack the mirror behind me because of his clumsiness. He wrapped himself hastily and thrust into me with much speed, my body arching into his.

"Make it quick," I whispered, my fingernails clawing into his forearms.

He took less than thirty thrusts into my body. The wine haze allowed me to stay in the zone even though I couldn't reach my orgasm. Once he came, he brought me down quietly onto the floor, both of us panting, his in broken release and mine in utter confusionThere was a comfortable awkwardness between us as we adjusted our clothes, our fingers terrified of touching each other while our fluids mingled on our bodies.

"I'm sorry," he murmured.

Shaking my head, I replied, "It happens."

His gaze wandered up to the skylight. The lighting was so oddly pleasant for such a rushed encounter.

"I am marrying her next week," he shared quietly.

Chuckling, I turned to him and asked, "Is that so?"

"We've been together for seven years. It has to be done," he responded.

"Now that is exactly how I want my future husband to think of me when I get married: '*It has to be done.*'"

"It's not like that. I do love her," he said.

"If you loved her, we wouldn't have done this," I said before standing up and adjusting my makeup in the mirror.

"You don't understand," he said, picking up the hint and adjusting himself. "We've been so stressed with this wedding, and I just can't make her happy right now. I know that once the wedding is over, we will be able to be happy again."

While shaking my head sadly, I saw the loneliness return to his onyx gaze. After nodding, I whispered, "Let me give you a piece of advice: Don't marry someone to keep from being alone. Marry them because you can't imagine your life without them. You owe it to yourself and to her to do that."

"Will I see you again?" he asked quietly.

"Downstairs," I replied. "However, I don't believe you will ever again after today. It wouldn't be right."

He agreed and reached for me again. I took a step back and reached for the door handle. I shook my head and walked out first. We had been gone for less than ten minutes; no one had missed us yet.

A week later, I was waiting in the drive-through line at my favorite Starbucks and glancing at my Facebook app. When it finished reloading, I saw a series of photos that our mutual friend had posted from his magical wedding day. To everyone else, they appeared happy and full of love. Yet when I looked at his eyes, I saw that he was still trapped in loneliness. "Oh well," I said to myself before turning off my phone and driving away, our shared brokenness left in the wind.

XV: Novels that Turn into Movies that Turn into Expectations

Christmas is my favorite holiday season. For just about thirty-five to forty days, I get swept up in the romantic and festive cheer that is reinforced by classic songs and Hallmark movies. For the month of December, there is generally a smile etched on my face that I can't take off—even in the most stressful of moments.

One of my favorite traditions is selecting our Christmas tree of the year. You need precision and purpose when you choose your tree. There are the predetermined measurements and placements that you select within your home for where this thirsting life-form will reside. Then you must conduct the necessary research of the local tree farms within your area and identify what tree food is necessary for your selected tree to stay moist and vibrant throughout the winter holiday. Once your preparations are made, you can explore the different tree farms. You must take the time to visually assess each tree, study the branches and needles for scent and moisture, take in the size and shape, and then listen for if the tree calls to you. If your tree has called to you, you will be overcome with a sense of peace and acceptance. Identify the tag and then bring it to the register. Select any additional lights or ornaments that you may need, and then be prepared to load your chosen tree into your truck and drive away.

It should have been a simple romantic escapade. Taking an annual tradition and sharing it with a tall and handsome friend-that-can-turn-lover is storybook romance. He had fit me into his incredibly intense schedule, and I offered him coffee and a wink. It should have been the launchpad into holiday superstardom that would have made a story of lovers for future generations. It should have been, and yet the hilarity that follows ensured that it truly wasn't the holly, jolly Christmas I had expected.

The air of Los Angeles burned with a tinge of smoke and anxiety. Southern California was literally on fire. From the Santa Barbara hills to the 405 freeway, the dryness of California went aflame and began torching the historic landmarks of Santa Barbara and Los Angeles Counties. The flames were able to take hold due to the rambunctious Santa Ana winds. Hot winds swirled and created dust storms that created suffocating heat and blurred vision for pedestrians and drivers in every driving element. While the songs on the radio cried out for white Christmases, gray ash descended from the sky, clogging air-conditioning systems in apartment buildings, stores, and schools throughout the San Fernando Valley. Safety policies were enacted that caused students and employees of every occupation to keep from work in order to ensure their safety. Freeways were closed, and first responders were on constant rotation to put out the flames.

In an evening of spontaneous romance among the burning chaos, I had reached out to my handsome truck-driving friend for an evening of Christmas-tree selection. We met at a Starbucks where I came out with a mocha and cocoa. It would have been the perfect beverage if we weren't baking in 85-degree weather. Our drive was filled with pleasantries; I gained information about his day while I shared my concerns about my students who were stuck in the fire zones.

We arrived at the first tree lot. When he parked the truck, I realized that his work equipment was in the back. Immediately filled with nervousness and guilt, I began backpedaling and offering to come back another time. With a kind smile, he urged me to find a tree and to call him when I was ready.

With a skip in my step, I started looking at the trees, going through the Douglas and grand firs, debating the textures and designs of each tree in the five- to six-foot ranges. I had selected our family's tree. He was beautiful. Approximately six feet tall, this Douglas fir was perfectly balanced and raised in the Washington mountains. Its core didn't feel dry, and its branches contained an acceptable balance of moisture and fragrance. There was a tree stand nearby that I chose to purchase along with this tree. After taking a nearby cart, I went through the store and selected new lights and ornaments for the tree.

As I waited in line, I began mentally picturing the night ahead. We'd load up the tree in the truck, drive it to my apartment, and set it in the front corner by the door. As I would balance the tree and take in its presence, I'd warm up some spiked cocoa and invite him to stay and decorate the tree with me. With classic songs playing in the background, we'd take our time while decorating the tree, tear up when we lit the tree for the first time, and share some time together on the couch, enjoying the music and dim lighting. I'd reach over and grab his hand gently, his blue eyes would meet mine, I'd bite my lower lip gently, he'd lean in ever so slowly, and then—

"Ma'am, I'm ready!" the cashier said, taking me out of my mental escape.

I presented the Home Depot employee with my basket of purchases. I brought out my checkbook and began writing out a check to the store. I knew that payday was a day away, but I couldn't wait to pick out my handsome tree with a truly wonderful man.

I handed the check to the cashier and prepared my bags to leave. Suddenly, with bright and bold red letters, "Check Declined" appeared across the screen.

"Um . . .," the cashier said to me awkwardly.

"That's impossible," I replied. "Can I please try again?"

"Sorry, one check, one attempt," he responded apologetically.

"Can you give me a minute?" I asked, embarrassed.

"Of course," he replied.

With the speed of a thousand camels going to Bethlehem, I went to my online banking portal and found out that my account was just short of the amount needed for the tree. There was no way that I could walk out of this store with the tree I wanted with the amount that was in my account. With sad eyes, I turned to the cashier and informed him that I would not be completing the purchase. His remorseful "Merry Christmas" response felt like a bullet to my holiday-spirited heart.

As I made my way toward the exit doors, I was reminded that my friend was eagerly waiting for me and my little boy tree in his truck. It was too soon for me to share with him that money complications were the reason that I didn't have the little boy tree or any decorations. I had until the rings of our phone transmission to come up with a realistic reason for why my hands were empty.

"Hey!" he answered with a smile in his voice.

"The trees are ugly," I said in a vomit-style reaction.

"What?" he asked, confused.

What the fuck just came out of my mouth?! "Um, yeah, none of them were right." The words were stumbling out of my mouth.

"It's okay," he replied. "I found three other lots that we can look at. We will find your tree."

My heart was filled with romantic gratitude and sizzling panic. *How the fuck am I going to pull this off?* I thought to myself. I climbed into his truck, smiled gently, and allowed him to drive us to our next destination.

My fear of him learning my financially complicated secret left me acting like a complete and utter mess. With each perfect tree, I'd identify the oddest reason for why it wasn't the right fit. "It's too tall!" "It's wide." "The branches are dying. Can't you feel them dying?"

With patience that rivaled the one possessed by the guards outside Buckingham Palace, he took me to three other tree farms, my anxiety spiking and my tears waiting behind my eyes because of my shame. After apologizing, I shared that none of the trees were the perfect fit. Yet the ones he selected were truly magnificent. They would have been perfect additions for the holiday season, but I was financially worthless.

With a heavy sigh, he turned to me and asked me if I was ready to go home. With a sad smile, I nodded, and we made our way to his truck. Bing Crosby's gleeful voice couldn't bridge the conversation or mood between us. Our night was ruined, and my own fears and embarrassment kept me from getting close to him.

He pulled into the alleyway and put his truck into park. In my mind, I had expected us climbing all over each other, my mouth biting into his long neck while his large hands fondled my aching breasts. Yet as we sat in silence, I was terrified of even our pinky fingers touching.

"Well," we both said, and then we chuckled.

"I'm sorry," I apologized immediately. "I know you have been working a lot, and tonight feels like a waste of time."

"You'll know when it's the one," he responded.

My blood turned to ice as I turned to meet his gaze. He was looking straight ahead, his focus on everything beyond where we were. "What?" I asked.

"The right tree," he replied. "You are very particular about the right tree."

My heart breaking within, I knew that we were no longer talking about trees. Neither my pride nor my heart was prepared to be honest about my financial blunder. Both conflicting entities were willing to risk him leaving this alley and never coming back instead of appearing incompetent and vulnerable. Nodding, I agreed and reached for the doorknob. "Thank you," I whispered.

"Of course," he replied.

Moving to his side, I took a moment to look at his strong face. His kindness and patience were etched with exhaustion and concern. I knew he was analyzing the situation as much as I was. I leaned forward to kiss him gently on his lips, only to be met with his scruffy cheek. I moved back as if I was struck by lightning, and he turned to me with a sad smile and wave. I watched as his black truck rolled down the alley, my holiday expectations going away in the ashy wind that followed him.

The romantic expectation that I set for myself died along with the thousands of trees that were burned during the December fires. I wish I could say that I went back and purchased the first handsome tree that I had discovered with my handsome friend. Instead, I was plagued with emotions of disappointment and inadequacy and didn't make my way back to the Christmas-tree lot. *Maybe next year*, I thought to myself as I packed away the winter decorations.

XVI: Orgasms and the Games We Play to Get Them

Release.

Release brought upon internal tension, the biting of the lower lip, intentional thrusts toward the target of knee-shaking and mind-numbing bliss.

I was in dire need of an orgasm.

There was only so much that my red-and-black lace-patterned vibrator could provide me.

I was in need of a stranger that I wouldn't have to encounter again. I wanted him to be tall with broad shoulders and a whiskey-tinged smile, his long hair demanding my hands to tug his silken tresses. The five-o'clock shadow along his jawline would irresistibly scratch my inner thighs as he feasted on my dripping flesh. He'd look at my deliciously tortured body with a wolfish grin as his calloused fingers fucked me, and his greedy tongue would lap me up as if he'd die without more of my essence.

That is what I needed—an evening of pure primal connection that never needed to resurface again.

I knew everything I needed to accomplish the next day. Our encounter didn't need to last more than two hours. After we were finished, I'd play nice and stay until he fell asleep. I often don't go for talkers, so sleeping comes rather easily.

The deadweight of his arm across my body would serve as my cue to begin my secret-agent-style escape from his room. Slowly I'd lift his arm so I could maneuver my torso away from his body. I'd spend no more than two minutes on lifting his arm and shimmying out of his grasp. Once I was free, I'd take a look at the path of where our clothes fell and take note of how quickly I could grab each item before finally leaving his sleeping quarters. My record is eleven seconds. It pays to prefer flip-flops and sandals. Silence is simpler to control when one deals with carpeted floors instead of wooden ones. While wood floors are significantly easier to maintain, they often creak and alert light-sleeping lovers of your impending escape. With swift movements and direct lines to the bedroom door, I can access the doorway and silently escape his room without notice. With the door closed behind me, I could choose to get dressed in his hallway or in the bathroom. If I have more time, the bathroom is always best for me; I can use it to freshen up and adjust so I don't look like I just got fucked senseless and was without fashionable awareness.

It was a good trade in my opinion—a quick evening of shared passion and orgasms with no obligation to follow up or make contact ever again after the shared experience. Having to return home each evening to a family full of responsibilities and daily management tasks made my escape strategy much more important to master. My early twenties were no time to fall in love or to sustain a long-term relationship. There was simply no room for someone in my life except for a solitary night of shared physical release.

There is one evening that comes to mind where my need for sexual escape was high. I had been casually seeing a wonderful man who had the sexiest smile I'd seen since Dennis Quaid's. His blue eyes were full of mischief, while his six-foot form commanded the attention of any woman who was in a room with him. However, after three months of fun and games, he told me that he believed I wasn't as invested in our encounters as he was and that he wanted someone who would give him everything that he needed.

His comments bruised my pride. I was giving him everything I could with my borrowed time. Yet if he couldn't see what I was doing for him, fuck him! I didn't need him. Clearly, he didn't understand everything I had to balance in my life. It didn't help that this split happened just before the holidays—the time of year when my heart goes to mush and begins imagining tales of happily ever after.

I was a woman in need of an orgasm and a reminder that my escape plan was mutually beneficial for both parties involved. I had been invited to attend an ugly-sweater party that was going to be hosted by one of my fellow undergraduate friends. I was incredibly grateful that I made vibrant and party-loving connections at Sacramento State University. Weekends were filled with nonsensical choices, music, and laughter heightened by the consumption of alcohol and other substances.

My objective was simple: Find a friend of a friend, exchange flirtatious banter with him, suggest that we step away for some time alone, chase no more than three orgasms between the two of us, and then drive home alone so I could prepare to help my grandma with Christmas shopping the next morning.

That evening, I arrived at the party. Classic Christmas songs mixed with hip-hop tracks were being blasted by the complex-nominated and drunk college DJ. Many of my friends had pregamed throughout the day. There were college boys from local apartments participating in a heated Santa-themed beer-pong tournament, their participant board pinned up in the living room as the scantily clad hostess kept track of the winners and humiliated losers of the festive event. The ladies of the party were scattered throughout the unit. Some were cheering on their male companions as they competed, some sat on the couch and shared bottles of wine and gossip, and others danced on the makeshift dance floor that was created by moving the kitchen table to the other side of the dining area.

I entered the festive doorway and was greeted with sloppy kisses underneath the mistletoe and some homemade eggnog that could paralyze a reindeer. After downing my first cup, the hostess refilled my holiday glass and introduced me to people that I hadn't met yet.

While I was exchanging pleasantries, my sexual objective remained at the forefront of my mind. I needed to find an available target soon.

With laughter and a cry of defeat, my gaze turned to the beer-pong table. The loser of the current round caught my attention. He was impressive in size and wore a holiday version of the Minnesota Vikings football jersey. He wore a backward hat and dark-blue jeans. He turned and met my inquisitive eyes, winked at me, and moved to scratch his name off the tournament board.

Yep, he's the one.

I strategically made my way to the kitchen to refill my eggnog. Within fifteen seconds, he was beside me at the refrigerator, grabbing a beer from one of the packs. With a smile, I turned and took a sip of the strong beverage in my hand.

"Nice loss," I said.

Smiling, he replied, "Yep. I sure showed them some Minnesota pride."

"Ah, Midwest?"

"Yep. I'm flying out tomorrow morning. I just came by for some drinks before I started packing."

Jackpot! "Going home for the holidays?"

He nodded; he then took a drag from his beer and responded, "Yep. Always good to be with the family."

Stepping toward him, my tone became more predatory than casual. "When do you need to get out of here?"

Leaning down, he whispered in my ear, "An hour, tops."

Biting my lip with happy anticipation, I grabbed him by the hand and led him up the stairs of the crowded apartment. My friend had given me a quick tour of the unit before she became too intoxicated.

We entered the bedroom that kept the coats and purses of all the guests. After locking it behind us, we latched on to each other, feeling starving need and the necessity for quickness. His jersey came off first, my hands trembling over his defined pectoral muscles and tattooed arms. Wetness pooled in my panties as his hand unzipped my pants. I moved backward and started to fall onto the bed. Before I could finish falling, he spun me against his tall form and held me against him, his firm cock pressing against me with pulsating need. He removed himself temporarily to throw the jackets and purses to the floor, and then he tossed me onto the spring-filled mattress. I lay back, enjoying the view of his strong form crawling up my body. He left nibbles and kisses upon my skin as he worked to turn me on and leave me panting for more.

I am always a sucker for gripping onto hair. I was trying to remove his cap when he gripped my wrist and met my eyes with a commanding tone. "The hat stays."

Enjoying the move of dominance, I nodded and pulled his face close to mine for more heated kisses, our tongues fighting for dominance while our bodies ground into each other.

His lips escaped mine as he made his way down my body. Arching my back, I relished the feeling of his mouth on my body, his moans sending vibrations through my skin and directly to my core. I was soaking in anticipation and needed him to take my panties off with much more urgency.

It was during a flash of momentary frustration that I realized his moans held a musical melody within them. My eyebrows arched as my eyes were closed; I tried to decipher if I was hallucinating or if the music from downstairs was affecting my current state of mind.

He continued to move farther south, and the tone of his humming became much more intentional. *Is he humming?* I thought to myself. As I listened to the tune, I realized the tone wasn't one that was part of the holiday collection in my memory bank. This was much more . . . theatrical?

Reaching down, I tapped his back with my festive acrylic nails. "Um . . ."

"You like that?" he asked, his mouth moving to my zipper to release me from my navy prison.

"I have to ask," I began, my thumb rubbing up against his reddened ear. "Are you humming to yourself?"

With a smile, he went above me, his forearms cornering me and making me meet his gaze. He was beaming as if I solved a secret riddle that he had purposely left for me. "Have you seen *Fiddler on the Roof*?"

I felt as if a bucket of spine-chilling ice crashed over me, my need for sexual release running farther from my clit with each hurried heartbeat. "What?" I asked.

He sat up, his arms and hands motioning in festive theatrical gestures. "Tradition! Tradition!"

Oh hell no! I thought to myself. Shaking my head, I rolled off the bed and was desperately looking for my hideous red-and-green holiday sweater. "Oh my god!" I angrily whispered to him.

"What?" he asked, genuinely confused as to why I was moving farther and farther away from him.

"Were you really getting hot and bothered over the opening song of *Fiddler on the Roof*?!" I asked in a demanding tone.

"It is a very compelling story that is full of romance and dramatic interludes!" he argued.

My anger and confusion were racing through my mind as if Santa's reindeer stumbled into a barrel of catnip and cocaine. I couldn't think clearly, and my secret-agent escape plan transitioned to a run-and-leave-immediately plan. "FYI," I said as I struggled to button up my sweater in the dark, "if you're about to go down on a woman, you need to leave the show tunes at home. I can't think of anything more unattractive!"

"Fine!" he replied. "I guess I'll find a lady who wants some culture in the sack!"

Making my way to the door, I yelled back, "Culture?! You're from Minnesota, you ass!"

While making my way down the stairs, I realized that I looked like a complete mess. None of the buttons were aligned, my hair was flipped to the opposite side of my part, and my lipstick was smeared across my cheek.

My friend was engaged in his round of the beer-pong tournament when he saw my appearance and began laughing hysterically. After flipping him off, I nodded to all my friends, grabbed my car keys, and exited the apartment with as much dignity as I could muster.

I used the twenty-three-minute drive home to process the failure of sexual gratification that I encountered. Instead of anger and disappointment, I began laughing in desperate hysteria and replayed the comedy of errors in my mind. At the Riverside exit, I retrieved the makeup wipes from my purse and began removing the holiday coloring from my face. Tomorrow would be another day full of chaos and laughter. While this evening proved to be a failure, I knew this epic horror story would bring me laughter for many nights to come.

XVII: Proximity Theory

Crash!

My head was protected by the ugliest helmet ever created when a beige truck hit me while I was on my bicycle and making my way to Sacramento State University for my mandatory English class. I lay on the pavement, looking up at the scorching sun and asking myself how I got there. Other students began walking around me. I could hear the spindle of my bicycle spinning.

The driver of the truck rolled his passenger window down so he could look at me. I could feel his panicked gaze as he looked me up and down. I struggled to pick myself up. He yelled out the window, "Hey! Sorry I hit you! But I gotta catch the light!" In a flash, more correctly with the green lights at 65th and Folsom Blvd, the truck driver drove away, heading for his intended destination.

My body was filled with adrenaline. *I have been hit by a truck and am perfectly fine.* After looking down at my mangled bicycle, I adjusted my handlebars, climbed back on, and knew I'd be fine even if I went to class. *People get hit by trucks every day. I'm not wasting an absence for this hiccup.*

As I rode my bike, I could hear it struggling to roll correctly. What was once a smooth ride was now bumpy and full of bounce. I felt like Indiana Jones when he was on the back of his motorcycle in *Temple of Doom* more than a student heading to a class that I could care less about.

I began to notice the stares. When you survive being hit by a truck, people tend to take notice. Their looks of shock and awe were quite flattering. They whispered among each other as they looked me up and down. Yeah, my broken bike and I were going to be CSUS legends.

When I approached the bike rack, I realized that my bike was no longer able to roll smoothly into the port. The wheel was now shaped into a pentagon-like form. Chuckling, I brought the bike lock out of my backpack and attached it to the side of the transportation-locking apparatus.

While stretching my neck and back ever so slightly, I heard the ringing of my phone. I glanced down with a smile, knowing how much my mom loved our morning chats.

"Morning, Mama."

"Morning, baby girl. How's your morning going?"

"You know what? It's been quite eventful!" I said with a jovial tone.

"Really? Tell me about it."

"Well, I was headed to school on my bike and was a little hung over—"

"No shock there," my mom interjected with a chuckle.

"Well, when I crossed in front of the gas station, a truck driver wasn't paying attention, and he hit me with his truck."

Startled, she interrupted me. "Wait, you were hit by a truck? Rach, you need to get to a hospital!"

"Mom, I'm fine. I'm full of energy. My bike can be fixed, and I can't afford an absence in this class. I don't want to retake it."

"Rach, that energy is called shock. You can have internal bleeding, a concussion, or broken bones."

"Ugh, why do you have to be so dramatic?" I asked, exasperated.

My lungs began to struggle with taking in air, but I was not about to tell my mom that she could be right. "Mom, I'm telling you I'm fine. Maybe I am viewing this wrong and I hit the truck!"

"Really? You rode straight into a truck?" my mom asked sarcastically.

"Yep! Maybe I am just a hunter for cars and trucks and my bicycle-riding persona is hungry for oil and car blood."

"Okay, my daughter, the ultimate avoider, needs a mental-health check as well as a physical checkup."

My mom paused to gather her words. I could imagine her eyebrow raised with concerned judgment and her beautifully curved hands scratching the same spot behind her ear that she reached for during times of high stress. "I'm calling your grandparents and asking them to take you to the hospital."

I froze in panic as my body stopped walking up the stairs of Lassen Hall. My grandparents were the best human beings in the whole world. They helped everyone for any reason. However, they were getting older, and I didn't want them traveling to Sacramento for no reason. I was perfectly fine. "No, Mama! Don't call them! You know that they have so much going on right now—"

"Too late. I'm dialing on the landline. Get yourself to a hospital now, Rachel Renee. I mean it."

Well, fuck! I looked down at my hands and noticed some blood. Looking up and down my arms, scratches seemed to appear on them like magic. Looking down at my ribs, blood began oozing beneath my shirt, staining my black-and-white striped dress with a pop of red. I moved my hand through my hair and was greeted with more blood.

Looking up, I saw my young professor looking at me with a more pale tone to her face than usual. With shaky legs, I walked toward her with a nervous smile.

"Oh my god!" she murmured.

"So, I was hit by a truck—"

"No shit!" she shrieked. "You're going to the campus's urgent care now!"

I attempted to say, "I'm fine," but I got hit by a wave of exhaustion, or was it organ failure? I really couldn't connect my thoughts at that moment.

"Don't worry about the absence. Just get checked out! Do you want someone to walk you?" she asked.

"No, I can take myself. Thank you for understanding."

She shook her head in disbelief as she watched me walk toward the medic station, which was a half mile away.

When I arrived at the urgent care, I was greeted with surprised looks and panicked gazes. According to the doctors, I was the first student in Sacramento State history to come to their urgent care after being hit by a truck. I was given every test they could give me as well as my choice in lollipops. Fortunately, I left the urgent care with a few stitches and a concussion. They recommended that I take some time to rest and maybe find a hot tub so I could ease my aching muscles.

That hot-tub recommendation set up the next ten months of my life in the greatest whirlwind of youthful mistakes.

That evening, I met a boy who would become the first to win over my heart and would later participate in the breaking of pieces within me that I didn't know existed. I was attracted to how different he was from me; he was my polar opposite in many ways. I was short and curvy. He stood nearly seven feet tall and had limbs so long that they could wrap around the earth. His voice spoke of adventures and drunken, wild nights that colored my world with a vibrance I had never known. He was inviting, he was charming, and he held a confidence within himself that I couldn't help but need to surround myself with.

We began our friendship in the hot tub after I witnessed him and his friends standing upon the concrete wall that protected our complex from the light rail. On the wall, he and four others decided to pull down their swim shorts and moon the speeding train, their immaturity and humor confusing my pained brain. Yet as they ran with laughter to the hot tub, I couldn't help but laugh along with them.

They lived in the complex in multiple rooms throughout the building. Ranging in ages from eighteen to thirty, these four boys shared their introductions with flirtation and humor. It was quick to see that they all valued beer, women, and *South Park*. While I had met several people as I attended my first month at university, I had yet to meet such a vibrant group of young men.

Through the vast conversations, the tallest one found his way

71

beside me, his long arm wrapping around me in a motion of comfort and charisma. Between the dull pain that my body was in and the ease of the moment, I didn't ask him to remove his arm. Instead, I leaned in closer against his body and rested my head upon his chest. We talked for hours, sharing where we were from and what brought us to the hot tub that night. None of the boys could believe that I was hit by a truck earlier that day. I received a free beer for my victory and numerous offers to escort me to my class the next day since none of them wanted me to walk alone. The tall one offered me a ride in his truck. I have always been a sucker for tall trucks.

It was hard to believe that hours had passed with our visit. Three of the four boys left after the hour passed one, yet the blue-eyed tall one and I stayed until my fingertips began to prune like California raisins. It was hard to believe that someone so full of life and adventure could be my neighbor. As we walked toward my loft's doorway, I was taken by surprise when he gently turned me and went in for a kiss. It was the contact needed for Cupid to shoot an arrow of interest through my heart and keep me anchored to this tall man for the foundation of my formative years.

He was three doors down from my room, yet we seemed to spend all our time together. When we weren't driving throughout Sacramento County to seek new adventures, we were walking to classes, going to parties, and texting until our phones burned with heat and excess energy. Our lives were intertwined to the point of suffocation. Through the comfort of vodka and tequila, young passion began to ignite and burn a path of blurred days and long nights.

I began to adopt aspects of his personality as my own. It was easier to assimilate to what he wanted because he was interesting and held an investment in our future together. I quickly realized that he didn't like it whenever I strayed from the vision of his dreams, and it was more important for me to keep him in my life rather than to stay who I was when he met me. I began learning languages because he wanted to travel the world. I started drafting five-year plans that included investing in real estate properties in multiple parts of the world so that we would have options wherever we escaped to. I expanded my career choices from my original law-enforcement dream to becoming an attorney because I could build a stronger financial future for the two of us if I became one. Being nearer and more important in his life meant that I needed to change; I felt that he was worth me changing my hopes and dreams.

I had stated earlier that vodka and tequila were important to us. However, as our time together progressed, our dependence on these substances grew. It came to a point where I didn't recognize his scent without the aura of alcohol on his skin. He would fill bottles of water with clear alcohol and take them to class so that he could get through the lectures. Our dates together went from the comforts of Old Spaghetti Factory to twenty-four-hour Mexican-restaurant drive-throughs and the McDonald's dollar menu. Our "I love you's" went from being melodramatic, youthful forms of expression to acidic chains that held us together with obligation and convenience.

During the nights that were the most brutal and heartbreaking, he would always say he loved me. When he told me he loved me, it felt like the hardships were worth it. He *loved* me. He chose me. I ignored it when he told me we were both no more than a six on a scale that went up to ten and the passive-aggressive comments he would make in anger. I kept reminding myself that he said he loved me. I'd deny the looks he gave to other women, the nights he wouldn't come home, and all the canceled plans with my family. I would tell myself that he loved me and that our future together was going to be worth going through these challenges.

We had been together for eight months, and we were constantly together. My parents had invited me home for the weekend. We were supposed to go together. I had packed both of our bags. Yet the night before the six-hour drive, we got into a screaming, drunken fight about how I bullied him into every aspect of our life and that he needed time to be a man. He shared that I was suffocating, that I never wanted what he wanted, and that he needed to find himself. With injured pride, a bitter hangover, and a broken sense of confidence, I took the drive alone and went to the haven of the beach that I loved to call home.

With each mile separating us, I could feel anxiety and relief battling each other within my core. I had the freedom to listen to the music I wanted to listen to and to sing loudly or be silent. I was free. I began being comfortable with simply being me. I would smile as the randomized music delved into the iTunes library and sparked a varied rhapsody mixed with the classics of Elton John and George Strait. I knew each word, each riff, and each growl of male musical ownership. I felt my soul finding itself once again in the healing power of musical nostalgia.

Just as quickly as my soul found relief, I found my eyes welling with tears and my hands shaking in fear as his dozens of texts came through my phone at the rest stop. The list of his demands was endless. He needed to know where I was, and he wanted to know who I was with. He was angry, and he was missing me. It was an array of chaos that I had caused by leaving. Bile rushed up my throat, and I couldn't find a trash can fast enough. The curb became the home of the churning vomit. I was hundreds of miles away, yet he seemed to be my shadow.

The curve of Avila Beach on the 101's southbound freeway was where I rolled down the window and took a healing breath of salty ocean air. The cleansing mist filled my lungs, and the shaking of my hands began to ease. I couldn't keep the smile off my face as I made my way toward the signless town of Grover Beach, where my parents were waiting for me with hugs and a home-cooked meal.

The weekend served as a needed rehabilitation of my spirit. I became truly unplugged from my life in Sacramento and started rediscovering who I was and who I wanted to be. Through loud, passionate arguments on the beach with my mother and early-morning coffee chats with my dad, I started getting an image of what I wanted for my life and who I wanted to share it with. I knew that I was young and had so much that I wanted to accomplish. I knew that I needed to separate myself from the relationship I was in and begin rediscovering who I was because I was pretty great. I was funny. I was sexy. I was worthy of someone who loved me for who I was. I was worthy of a partner who viewed me as a wanted person in their life and not a punishment.

I wish I could say that I returned to my apartment, called him over, and broke up with him. I wish I could say that I gave him a passionate speech about loving myself and that his alcoholic tendencies wouldn't hurt me anymore. I wish I could say that I held firm to my principles and walked my path strongly and independently.

Instead, when I returned to my apartment, he was waiting for me with a bottle of wine and words of him missing me. He held me in his arms, and I knew that this weekend retreat was needed in order to bring fresh energy to our relationship.

When I returned, our magnetic energy brought us dangerously closer together. Our actions no longer burned with passion but with desperation. The fire was fueled by accusations, jealousy, and substance abuse.

It took him walking away from our plans to get an apartment together and leaving the country to find himself and his passion for international culture for us to make the break we desperately needed. I barely recognized myself in the mirror as I cried into my beach-themed pillows and sang along with Lady Antebellum; I approached my first devastating romantic heartbreak with chocolate and wine.

Weeks after he left, I took a moment to return to the hot tub, my feet stepping into the warm water with caution and memory. It would take many more nights before I could go to the poolside without sadness or longing beside me. As our days and distance became cemented with permanence, he no longer served as my lifeline for happiness.

It hasn't been easy, moving on from the fractured breaks within me that came from this first relationship. It is with a degree of shame and embarrassment that I admit that I still possess triggers within my heart that keep me from moving forward completely. Yet with time, love, and distance, I know I'll find my way.

XVIII: Questioning all
that come into our path

Quivering lips, thighs and minds
Can't break the concrete that
Keeps you from me

Unfortunately, I am surrounded by
Warm and cruel fire
Each step closer burns my ripe flesh

Escaping the prison I have created
Is what I say I desire
What I want more than anything

Still your eyes beckon for
My courage, my presence
From across our miles long divide

Tried and true
You're waiting for me with utmost integrity,
Fidelity and selflessness

Insecurity and poisoned scars
Prevent me from believing your truth
You have done nothing to make me doubt your intentions

Only it is the pain of before
The blinding tears, the thickening blood, the grotesque gold bile
That reminds me of what you can do

Not only what you can do
But what you want to do
What you will eventually do

In a matter of moments
You will crush the demons
That guard my broken spirit

Ignoring the roaring drums of my heart
The fierce grip of my hands
The vicious words from my tongue

Granting you permission to possess my soul
Assure me of your undying love
Then abandon me just the same as the others before you...

XIX: Romance Is Dead (RK Arts)

XX: SCARS

Scars
Aren't they beautiful?
The evidence of experience and endurance
The way the new skin glistens with endless shine as it blends
with existing tissue
It's roughened texture lifted ever so slightly
Never to truly assimilate with the body
But to exist as a reminder of once was.

Scars are the proud war wounds of moments in time,
My clumsy form covered from head to toe,
From the chicken pox mark slightly off center between my
eyebrows
To the scattered patterns on my knees
Produced from public intoxication, a not-so-missing purse and
a mysterious construction site outside Shady Lady Saloon on my
twenty-first celebration of life,
My life has been colorful, beautiful and branded by consequences.

If scars are so beautiful, why are the ones wrapped around my
heart so suffocating?
It's as if no one can penetrate the thickened tissue,
A fortress born of foolish actions and cruel words.

This one is an old scar, painted by public humiliation and puberty.
I am never going to like you, ever.
He said that to me in line up in the fourth grade,
Our whole class waiting to walk down to the black top,
Our moms were friends,
I didn't see the slap coming from his wicked mouth,
Tears stinging my eyes as I prayed for escape.
I wouldn't cry here, my pride wouldn't allow it.
Yet I charged toward the 1991 station wagon as if my legs were
on fire,
When really it was my shattered heart.

Oh, this is a beautiful scar, jagged and oddly shaped.
Even the chunky girls need love.
I got this one on Bourbon Street at a bachelorette party,
Wearing a navy babydoll dress,
My breasts lifted ever so slightly,
I felt like a southern belle,
A charming blonde visitor to unknown majestic lands
Filled with jazz and voodoo,
Yet a hobo filled with vodka and pain crushed my fantasy.
I was defenseless, slashed by the thoughtless words of a human
who didn't know love or kindness,
Yet I was tarnished and beaten down,
Yes, an interesting scar indeed.

Oh, you see that one, don't you?
The one that hugs the four ventricles of my heart,
It's shaped demonic and poisonous.
It's okay, you can stare.
Remember, you are the one who fell in love with me. Not the other
way around.
Those were the last words I heard him say,
The boy who wrecked my innocence,
My romantic heart,

My joy.
He left to find himself,
I got lost in a sea of boys, alcohol and pain,
I believed I was over him and his rejection.
Yet he said this to me a year later,
The final gash that mauled my fragile heart.

How could pain hurt this much?
How could I be so blind?
How had he never loved me?
Why did I give him so much?
Why didn't he want me?

Oh no,
After all these years, that scar still bleeds,
The healing tissue digging deeper into my constantly beating
organ,
Blood struggling to navigate through the chambers.

Hey you,
You looking at me as if I am a wounded monster,
Can this monster be healed?
Can these scars be mended?
I'd give anything to make it so.

Would you like to try?
I can't promise you it will be easy,
You may even place new scars upon my form,
I'll try not to hide.

Wow, your scars are beautiful.
Would you like to tell me about them?

XXI: Thankful for Ghosts

For the past nine years, I had been struggling with sleep. I used to be such a sound sleeper—the kind that would fall asleep on any surface as long as I was horizontal. It was both a blessing and a curse. I would allow my eyes to drift and let myself escape to the fantasies conjured up by my mind. From bits and pieces of my daily life creating a semblance of normality for my unconscious mind to the visitors of wolves, forests, and limitless landscapes, my mind would rest for four to eight hours and surrender to the night.

However, the past nine years had made sleeping much more difficult. Mornings had become much worse during the most recent three. The dreams had been heavy with burdens and faded hopes. Tossing and turning, I couldn't help but wish for different circumstances and a life with less heartbreak and more passion.

Waking up was just as painful as sleep because loneliness occupied the space beside me. The right side of my mattress was much higher than mine, the memory foam not occupied with a consistent resident of its space. To make space, I pushed the bed against the wall, leaving me with a singular side table that possessed my beige lamp, novels, medications, reusable water gallon, and passion treasure bag. My friends told me that my bed was the most comfortable one they had ever lay on, yet I couldn't seem to find anyone who would stay there.

The physical absence wasn't the worst part of waking up alone.

No, it's the whispering burn upon my right hand and forearm from his missing weight. I could swear that I had a ghost of a memory upon my hands as I prepared to awake each morning. In recent years, before I opened my eyes, I rolled the fingers of my right hand from right to left, begging reality to allow me to feel the human pressure of his hand in mine. Gritting my teeth and squeezing my eyes, I prayed to find him there when I rolled over. Instead, I was greeted by the impatient set of brown eyes of my Tiger Lily, who was insistent on fulfilling her morning bathroom routine.

With a heavy sigh and a heavier heart, I sat up on my side of the bed and went through my morning routine. In a silent prayer, I asked God to be with my ghost partner, asked him to heal the burning in his own hands and arms, and asked him to forgive me as we continued to be apart.

My tortured sleep had started making lasting impressions upon my skin. While I was grateful to the miracle cleansers and creams of Rodan & Fields for capturing my youth for a longer amount of time than I deserved, I couldn't help but study the dark circles beneath my eyes and the wrinkles beginning to form around my lips.

Those are wrinkle lines, mija.

Chuckling, I could see her angelic ghost behind me as I brushed my teeth. Oh, how Rosie would have laughed at who I had become. She loved brushing the hair of her grandchildren, placing them safely upon a chair in the center of the tiny room and creating the most detailed braids with multicolored and seasonal hair ties and clips. My impatience would surrender to her five-foot frame, and I'd be her doll for as long as she wanted. With the patting of my hair and a kiss upon my forehead, she'd release me, and I'd run to catch up with Grandpa in the garage.

Oh, how those times were so long ago.

Shaking away her brown-haired ghost from my sleepy eyes, I returned to the preparation of my workday. After filling my gallon water jug; grabbing my container of mixed nuts, salami, and cheese; and kissing the pups good-bye, I made my way toward the distractions of my life. My beautiful job was blessed with people that filled my mind with purpose. My heart hoped to catch up with my settled mind.

As I drove through my local Starbucks's pickup window, I grabbed my morning venti quad-shot mocha with cinnamon powder and butter croissant. I promised myself that I'd give up 90 percent of my breads and grains, but I just love my morning pastry too much to give it up completely.

After taking a sip of the warm brown liquid of the gods, my Mustang, Sam Elliot, was ready to get me to work, which was forty-eight miles away, with power and style. After turning up the volume dial, I was greeted by the deep tones of Bob Seger, who asked me if he'd see me tonight on the downtown train. Escaping into the sounds of rock and soul, I hopped onto the 101 northbound, eager to chase my ghosts away as I embraced the multitude of tasks that awaited me.

However, the distractions of rock music and coffee weren't helping me this cold morning. The fog rolled in from the sea, its gray blanket leaving a mist upon each vehicle on the freeway. Each driver was assessing who was more aggressive and who was more timid as they made their way around Avila Cove.

As my windshield wipers brushed the preliminary mist away, I heard an all-too-familiar and very missed chuckle beside me. "Whatcha doin', kid?"

To my right, without any scientific explanation, my Grampa appeared in the passenger seat, wearing his brown slippers, navy-blue gym shorts, and a John Montero T-shirt that stated *"Same Shirt Different Day."* I turned my head and was greeted by his vibrant smile and laugh.

Shaking my head in disbelief, I replied with an airy breath, "Driving to work."

Nodding, he reached his large hand upon the dashboard and rubbed it proudly. "Hey, Rack, this is a nice rig you got here. You picked a good one."

My words failed me, the situation choking me with a burn of confusion and joy. He had been gone for so long, and now he was beside me and talking to me about my car of all things. I hated the idea of crying in front of him, but I had missed him. I couldn't even look at him for fear of my mind playing tricks on me.

When my voice box was again granted the freedom to speak, I asked, "Not that I am complaining, but why are you here?"

"You called us here, Racklee. You tell us."

"Us?" I questioned.

"Yes, us, mija."

My eyes widened as I felt a familiar hand upon my hair. Grandma had returned to me too. Her hair returned to its bold blackness, her fingernails perfectly manicured and soft pink. Her touch was something that my heart craved, her fingers making gentle curls through my messy, wet blond mane. "Your heart is troubled, mija."

"What's going on, kid?" Grampa asked again. This time, he used a more serious tone.

I redirected my gaze to the freeway. The traffic seemed to disappear as I breezed my way through San Luis Obispo. The left lane was Sam Elliot's home as he powered through the majority of workers who resided in the most popular city in the county.

"I don't know. It isn't your anniversary," I said, shaking my head in confusion.

"Your heart is troubled, mija. It is so broken." Grandma moved her hand to my shoulder, her grip tightening upon it. "Why would it be so broken, mija?"

Tears fell from my eyes before words could leave my lips. The burning salt betrayed my navy-blue eyeliner as I began seeing streaks of the bold minerals on my cheeks.

"It's always been broken," I replied.

"That's horseshit!" Grampa said with the traditional John Montero stubbornness. "My Racklee has had so much hope and has wanted to do so many things. But I agree with Grandma: You are a bit broken. What broke you, Rack?"

They knew what broke my heart, and I couldn't understand why they were pushing me to answer the question. Why would they need me to admit that losing them broke my entire sense of self? Why would they need to hear that without them, I didn't have any motivation to find someone, to fall in love, and to believe in happily ever after? How could I tell them that losing them changed everything; my heart breaking was only an example of collateral damage in a broken and darker world.

Sam Elliot approached the Cuesta Grade, which seemed to bring forth more fog. Gripping the steering wheel, I found myself powering through the seven-mile hill, gritting my teeth and wiping my tears away. Glancing back at Grandma, I could see her looking at Grampa with her knowing stare. No one had looks as powerful as Rosie. This was one of those moments.

"I don't know how to love without you two in my life!" I cried, my hot tears burning my throat, the tonsils hugging the airway with stubborn firmness.

Shaking his head, he reached over and grabbed my right hand, his thumb grazing the Montero family ring, which had been placed on my hand since I turned sixteen. "We are never without you, Racklee. We haven't left you."

"No, no! You are going to miss everything!" I shouted. "I can't even begin to tell you about the shame I feel from knowing that I didn't bring you my husband, didn't introduce you to your great-grandchildren, didn't do . . . didn't do . . ." I began to spiral, my hurt and regrets dominating my entire sense of self.

"Rachel, I need you to listen to me. We aren't missing any of those things. See, in heaven, we are allowed special moments like this, when we can drop in and watch all of you whenever we can. I know it doesn't feel like it, but we haven't left. We have even met your husband. I know my little great-grandchildren and the amazing things you will do with them on earth. We both know this because we are always with you, watching over you and praying for you."

"You can't mean that!" I cried, shaking my head, the tears making my voice unrecognizable. "How can I find someone who matches the great love you two had—the one that set the standard for what true love is?"

"Because when you meet him, Racklee, he is going to be your heart. It will be as if he has always been with you—just like how

I knew it with Tweety back then. It's a feeling. It's a heartbeat. You aren't broken. You just haven't opened your heart to accepting him yet."

The roar of the Mustang showed me that we were in the final mile of the grade, his power getting us through this last patch of fog and mystery. "How do I do that? How do I know?" I asked them.

Grandma smiled and leaned forward, her lips timid and gentle upon my cheek. "Trust him, mija. Trust him."

Sam Elliot started speeding down the hill, the speedometer going into the nineties instead of its typical high seventies to low eighties. "Shit!" I yelled, my foot gently pressing against the brake and my eyes darting around to spot any California highway patrolmen at the base of the hill.

Returning my car to its typical speed, I took a breath and looked around my car and found them gone. No longer was Grampa sipping my mocha beside me or Grandma touching my hair ever so gently. I was alone again.

Instead of being filled with the blackened pain of abandonment, I felt a lock being released within my chest. Without any effort from me at all, I found myself breathing easier. My eyes, though thoroughly damaged by my salty tears, were returning to their honey-brown state instead of living in the complexity of fractured emerald.

The remaining twenty-eight miles were effortless. My mind started to return to the tasks ahead; I reviewed lesson plans in my mind and thought about small groups and tasks that I needed to set up before my students arrived. This busywork always served as a distraction before, my heart hiding behind varied and countless tasks. With the lock releasing me from this brokenness, I became a better version of myself.

Parking the car in one of the staff spaces, I took a moment to review their words and presence. I had to memorize how they looked and what they said. I don't know if I will ever get that grace again. I was almost afraid to open my car door—afraid that opening the door would make me open my eyes in the safety of my bed and make me realize that all of this was a dream.

After opening the door, the brisk fall air chilled my bones. I opened my eyes and found myself still in the parking lot. "Thank you," I whispered. "I will love you forever."

While their ghostly visit brought divine wisdom to me, it also left behind a river of hope—a light that reminds me that there is so much more out there. I need to be open. I need to let go.

Maybe tomorrow morning, I won't wait to feel the burn against my right hand and forearm. Maybe this openness in my heart can break my habit of wanting someone who isn't here yet. Maybe, just maybe, we will have enough time to not miss him during the lonely moments.

I am not broken. Ghosts and angels helped pave my path to the future.

XXII: Untouchable

Mirror Mirror on the Wall,
What is it about me that makes me untouchable?

Is it my face?
Oh this too round face,
Double and Triple Chins can be seen at all angles...

Oh Lord, how is my eyeliner so uneven?
Shit, one eye looks almond shaped, the other round...

Is it this nose? Oh this pushed in nose I have!
I wish I could have belonged to wolf like people,
Those with perfectly angled faces and defined features.
Instead, I resemble my grandparents obsese senior King Charles
Cavalier,
Her breathing and waddle heard before ever seeing her come
down the walkway.

Is it the fact that my skin isn't warm in tone?
One glance in the sun's direction changes it form from pasty
white to painful red.
Who wants to touch a cherry tomato when you can caress sensual
suede?

Oh Mirror Mirror, maybe it isn't my face at all...

Do I smell?
Am I so nose-blind that I haven't caught the scent I give off of repulsion and disgust?
Body odor burning the nostrils of humanity and creatures county wide.

No, that can't be it. My chronic need to shower twice a day keeps that element in check.

If it isn't the face, if it isn't the scent...

Is it my voice? Oh God, is it my voice?
Some have told me that I sound like Drew Barrymore...
I've always taken it as a compliment.
Am I misguided?
Has it been a societal warning that this lisp and Californian accent are keeping all away from me?
Is my voice not one of a sensual mermaid luring her lovers to the shore for passion led destruction,
But instead, an awkward broken winged seagull choking on the cap of a water bottle, screeching and flapping about in hysteric distress.

Oh God, this horrible voice.

No, no Magic Mirror, those can't be the reasons why I am untouchable.

Maybe I have broken a cardinal rule of love in this or another life.
Maybe I betrayed my lover in a coven of witches and warlocks and have become cursed to live a life of solitude and unanswered prayers in this one...

Maybe it has nothing to do with a past life at all.

Maybe I got cursed in this life...

I can only think of one time I was intentionally rude to a boy at school.

I hung out with the wrong crowd for a time in Elementary
Learned false information from friends about what sex was
Would laugh with them when we talked about boys and girls
doing that to one another.
EW, why would they put that there? I'd ask naively.

Then there was a boy.
An awkward annoying boy.
He liked my friend.
She didn't like him.
I wanted her to think I was cool like her.

So I forged a note.
A misspelled, awkward note.
A note requesting sex from one student to another... in the third
grade.

Oh I thought nothing of the consequences.
No, this would keep us laughing for such a long time.

That is until I got called into the principal's office.
My mother's angry glare assaulting my senses when I entered
the room.
I got caught due to my inability to spell correctly.
Damn my dyslexia.

My consequences were fair.
Two weeks detention,
A public apology to my class for lying and starting rumors,
Two weekends in a row in my room with no television or privileges.

But maybe, magic mirror, those weren't my only consequences.

Maybe, because of my foolishness, God decided that wasn't a complete punishment.

Maybe because I wronged this awkward boy for no reason other than to be cool, he took away my chance at love in the future.

Maybe he built someone so special, so wonderful, so fulfilling for me...

Then my desperate attempt at popularity changed my destiny.

Yes, maybe I am untouchable because I made someone else untouchable.

So young and so dumb in the third grade I was.

How could I have known my choice would destroy my future?

Oh Mirror Mirror, have I found it? Is this the answer?
Am I suffering third grade consequences at thirty?

No... No... No...

Mirror, Mirror, please show me what I am missing.
I don't know why I am not someone men want to touch.
It has been so long. So painfully long since I have been wanted.
Desired.
Needed.

Mirror, Mirror, tell me what to say, what to do, what to be,
To connect with someone else,
To be loveable.
To be touchable.

Damn you, Magic Mirror
For you can't respond to me
I can only hear myself,
Caught in a trap of confusion and doubt,
My reflection not only the question, but the answer.

XXIII: Valentines
Are for Schmucks

Valentine's Day, once regarded as a holy day that honored a man who served as a symbol for engaged couples and bees, is now bastardized by capitalism and the two-dimensional societal embrace of token Hallmark love. It is a day that seems to always forget me; no chocolates or roses greet me with compliments of my beauty.

Instead, I have become dusty upon a shelf of isolation, wrapped in unflattering sweatpants and multiple pints of ice cream, washing down feelings of denial and stubbornness with the seductive liquor of Baileys Irish Cream. "I need no one," I kept telling myself. "There is more satisfaction in this pint of ice cream than in the company of a stranger."

Or so I have convinced myself.

The alcohol supported numbing traits that I needed to survive in academia. I was able to close myself off from the holiday and explore a vast world of serial killers and depraved sexual offenders. Through their senseless violence and complete disregard for human life, I skipped past feelings of hollow loneliness and wandered into feelings of gratitude for not being murdered on my most recent unsuccessful date and celebrating my critical eye for not falling into bed with the next globally recognized rapist or arsonist. *No, being alone will do just fine.*

I had a classmate in my sexual-offenders class who radiated joy and sass. Her brown hair was always in a different style, and her radiant smile would brighten the gloomiest room—even if we were exploring disemboweled women from 1970s cold cases. I was quite envious of her checker-print JanSport backpack, which gave off a cool vibe without being totally hipster.

We met in the back of the lecture hall. We'd call ourselves the Laptop Ladies. While our professor was incredibly interesting with his wide array of interviews and experiences, I was still a victim of a ten-minute maximum capacity for topic engagement. After a ten-minute window, I'd switch screens from my note pages to Facebook and explore the many adventures of family and friends instead of listening to yet another string of grotesque assaults.

It was in November that she confided to me that she had loved a broken man. He was her soul mate in all ways. He made her feel like she was more beautiful than Aphrodite and more sensual than Cleopatra. However, their three-year relationship was explosive. During my short companionship with her, they had broken up four times in two months. She didn't know how long they would last this time, she would tell me. However, if he proposed, she knew she couldn't say no. My rational mind couldn't understand the faith she had in him. The roller-coaster relationship that she talked about made me exhausted, and I just knew her from class. I couldn't even imagine being with someone so wild and irresponsible.

We were studying for an exam on the differences between disorganized and organized killers when she invited me on a belated Valentine's Day double date. Her boyfriend had four tickets to the Sacramento Kings versus Boston Celtics game. I had yet to attend an NBA basketball game, which was an item on my college bucket list.

She said his best friend would be the perfect match for me for the evening. He was an accountant who worked in the middle of downtown Sacramento; he could see the American River outside his office window. She said that he had given her boyfriend many chances to work at his firm, but he always turned them down in order to fight the system. I agreed to the date in order to fulfill my wish to attend a basketball game while not truly believing that much could come from this evening out on the town. Yet I was about to be taken on a journey that required a high level of patience, understanding, and flexibility in order to overcome the awkwardness ahead.

She and I met at a parking garage at the Sacramento State campus. Wearing a pair of acid-washed blue jeans and a purple V-necked sweater with matching lipstick, I had just finished googling the starting players for the Sacramento Kings so I didn't appear to be too much of a basketball novice. My friend decided to add more hints of romance to her outfit, exposing more leg and cleavage. I started getting anxious when our companions called her, asking for us to meet them at the arena. I was comfortable with a plan and an organized flow of the evening. This change to the routine made my shoulders tense. I grit my teeth to stop the building tension from reddening my already-pink cheeks.

"Darlin', relax," she told me. "They were closer to the stadium than the campus. Let's just go!"

While driving down the I-80 and dancing along to Baby Bash's "Cyclone" and 50 Cent's "In Da Club," I found myself getting excited for the evening ahead. The roar of my Mercury Mountaineer grounded my anxiety, my friend's smile assuring me that the evening would be filled with laughter and sparks of adventure.

After thirty minutes of following the instructions of minimum-wage traffic controllers, we found a parking lot and made our way toward ARCO Arena. I had recently attended the arena to take my cousin and his longtime girlfriend to see Disney on Ice. Through nostalgia and magic, Disney wrapped my heart in a blanket of love and warmed my spirit as the dancers glided through classic hits such as "Beauty and the Beast," "Once Upon a Dream," and "Part of Your World."

This evening's energy was quite different than the Disney night's. Rather than being swept up in Mickey Mouse's protective arms, the crowd roared with the essence of competition and alcohol. News vans lined the entrance of the arena as reporters inched their way toward the doors to catch a glimpse of the action that would begin within moments. The smells of alcohol and nacho cheese could be detected within a hundred-yard radius. No, romance and warm feelings were dominated by team loyalty and the heightened anticipation for the sounds and actions of basketball elite.

As we approached the box office, my eyes saw our male companions. It was hard to believe that two very different men could be neighbors, let alone lifelong friends. The accountant looked as if he had just arrived from his riverfront office. Dressed in a teal polo shirt and khakis, his hands fidgeted in his pockets. He seemed frustrated that his gold watch kept him from sinking his large balled hand farther into his pants. As I tried to meet his eyes, I couldn't tell if they were honey brown or light green. He turned away from me and stared directly into the setting sun. I raised my eyebrows, surprised and mildly concerned for his retinas as he didn't look away from the bright descent.

My friend's on-again boyfriend appeared to not have attempted to please anyone, let alone himself. In a dirty maroon sweatshirt and gray sweatpants, he looked disgruntled and impatient. After taking another drag of his cigarette, he stood up before shaking his head toward my friend with an air of resentment and displeasure. "You're late," he told us while throwing the remainder of his cigarette on the ground, putting out the embers with one of his torn black-and-white Converse sneakers.

In a heartbeat, I watched my friend's internal shine dim. The radiant and confident dancer who was just singing along to Trey Songz in the Mercury Mountaineer was gone, and the ghost of her jolly form stood before me. With a whine I had never heard before come from her lips, she responded to him, saying, "Baby, I'm so sorry. Don't be mad now, baby."

Walking up to him, she draped herself over his arm, her lips seeking the comfort of his neck. After shrugging her off, he gestured toward me. "Who's this?"

"This is Rach," she replied. "Rach, this is—"

"He's for you," her boyfriend interjected. He then shoved the awkward accountant toward me.

Startled by his uninvited entrance to my space, I stepped back and extended my hand. "It's a pleasure."

After he took my hand in his, I felt an abundance of sweat and grime. Forcing a smile, I worked to meet his eyes. Instead, he looked down at my shoes and motioned toward the box-office window.

"You've got the tickets, baby?" my friend asked.

"Yeah, yeah. Let's just get in."

While we walked toward the entrance, the boyfriend pulled out four tattered pieces of paper that appeared to be tickets from his wallet. When we got to the entrance, we were greeted by two ticket masters, who were eagerly listening to highlights of the game.

"Good evening!" the usher on the left said.

"Humph!" the boyfriend grunted before shoving the tickets toward the usher.

After raising his eyebrows, he gestured toward his colleague, who used his thin and fragile frame to block our entrance to the event.

I looked at the usher and asked, "Is there a problem?"

"Sir, I apologize, but these are event passes."

"Yeah, and we are going to the event," he responded to the usher while gesturing to the doorway.

"Yes, but, sir, you needed to have these event passes approved at least forty-eight hours before the event at the box office in order to select your seats and pay the additional service fees. Unfortunately, this game has been sold out for at least two weeks. If you see—"

"How the fuck is I supposed to know that?" he roared at the usher, his anger inflating his size and making him tower over the much smaller man.

Swallowing deeply, the usher replied, "Um, sir, if you look here at the directions on your event passes, it says right here—"

"I don't give a fuck about some fucking written directions. I am here to watch the fucking basketball game, and I am going to watch the game!" After grabbing his girlfriend's hand, he looked at both ushers and shouted, "You better be fucking taking us to our seats, bitch!"

Both ushers turned pale, yet they stood their ground and quietly motioned for security to intervene. "Sir, I apologize for this negative experience, but if you go to the box office, you can schedule your event with these passes."

"I'm not going to another fucking event, you piece of shit! I am going to this fucking basketball game!"

While looking to my right, I saw a security guard making her way to our group. My cheeks burned bright with embarrassment as I took a step back to take in the scene before me.

"Is there a problem here, gentlemen?" the woman asked. The security officer was impressive in size, her over-six-foot frame and cropped haircut setting a tone of dominance and control before she opened her mouth.

"Yes, ma'am," my friend replied. "These ushers won't accept my boyfriend's tickets."

Taking the crumpled papers into her hands, she took her time to read the materials before meeting his hot and aggressive gaze. "Sir, I apologize for the inconvenience. However, given the instructions on your passes, you needed to make seat selections at least forty-eight hours before your event—"

"Fuckin' bitch," he muttered while moving his body to face the security guard instead of the intimidated ushers.

"If you are interested in scheduling your next event with us at ARCO Arena, I can escort you and your party to the box office." Her tone remained professional and clipped as she ignored his tantrum.

"Yeah, I'll be fucking scheduling my event for tonight," he responded.

"I apologize, but the event for this evening is sold out, and we cannot accommodate that request," the security guard replied.

"What the fuck!" he shouted. He tore his arm away from his girlfriend's protective hold before thrusting his hands toward the sky with frustration and violent anger.

"Sir, you need to calm down." The security guard took a defensive stance, her hand hovering over the container of Mace strapped along her beltline.

"We are leaving," I interjected, walking several steps backward while longing for the safety of my vehicle.

"The fuck we are!" he shouted at me, his aggression aimed at me now instead of the security guard. "You aren't saying shit, bitch!"

"Sir, I will not ask you again to calm down!" The security guard took a step toward me to block the aggressive male.

He was clenching his fists with an animalistic rage, his eyes darting around as he tried to decide who he would inflict his pain upon: the ushers, the security guard, or my big mouth.

Taking a step forward to block him from the security guard, my friend put both of her hands upon her boyfriend's chest and began gentle vertical strokes to calm him down. "Baby, it's okay. Let's just go get some dinner. We can go another time. It's not worth this."

Shoving her hands away from his chest, he brushed past her and began walking toward the parking lot. My date quickly followed behind him without taking any stock into my plans or safety. Embarrassed, the girlfriend took the crumpled passes from the ticket ushers and apologized for the outburst. I thanked the staff and quietly followed my friend down the steep stairs of ARCO Arena, barely able to process the needless aggression that I bore witness to.

I looked at her and saw an array of emotions dance upon her face. Shame, embarrassment, confusion, disappointment, and sadness were just a few of the emotions that clouded her vibrant hazel eyes with tears. After taking her hand in mine as a show of solidarity, she shook her head and looked up with a broken smile. "Are you hungry?"

Torn between wanting to run away and wanting to stand by my friend, I shrugged my shoulders in response.

"We've got to eat, so let's eat!" After clapping her hands, she took strong, intentional strides toward my car. "BJ's!" she shouted.

I nodded and made my way toward the driver's seat, mentally preparing my escape route for the next section of this date.

I had been to BJ's Brewery on several occasions with family and friends. I appreciated the comfort of pizookies with the entertainment of ESPN, SportsCenter, and the NFL Network. Knowing that I would need to ease my tension relatively quickly, I decided upon ordering a glass of red wine when we sat down before receiving the menu.

There were many ways that this date could move forward from this parking lot to the restaurant and beyond. More likely than not, this would continue to be a shit show—a potentially record-setting disaster for the dating books. If that was the case, I could always text my cousins to call and help me fake an illness or death in the family to escape. If a more dramatic exit was necessary, I knew of the exit near the kitchen adjacent to the bathrooms. I would need to be strategic—bringing my purse, keys, and phone with me to the bathroom—in order for that exit to be successful.

Now if my date decided to stumble upon his personality in the isolated car ride with his friend, I knew a way to up the charm factor and find an exit with him. After plying him with necessary alcohols and appetizers, I could flirt my way toward an early exit, exchange phone numbers and kisses, and drive away without any obligation for further contact.

"What are you thinking about?" my friend asked me, taking me out of my planning mindset.

"Nothing," I replied. "You?"

"Nah, baby girl," she replied. "I'm just hungry."

"Good! I think our latest paper earned us a good Valentine's dinner."

"Right?" she responded with a smile. "Were you assigned bestiality or necrophilia?"

"Necrophilia. You?"

"Bestiality! Ugh, I had to make Jesse sleep outside the past few nights. I couldn't fool around with his beady little eyes staring at me so intently!"

Shaking with disgust and laughter, we made our way to the parking lot and were blessed by the parking gods with a spot at the front-section parking. After turning off my lights, I took another opportunity to adjust my makeup while looking at our male counterparts, who were waiting at the entrance. My date decided that the weather took a turn toward the cold and adorned his muscular arms with a gray cardigan. I was anxiously waiting for his Harry Potter glasses to appear and complete his stereotypical accountant appearance.

"He's a gin guy," my friend said.

"Who?" I asked.

"Your date. You would ease the tension if you surprised him by ordering for the two of you two gin and tonics."

"But I was going to get a—"

"Get the gin and tonics, Rach." Her tone was clipped and direct.

I raised my eyebrows and nodded. We exited the SUV and walked toward the doors. I watched waves of tension crash upon my date's shoulders. As he was as stiff as a cardboard box, I thought my presence was too stressful for my male companion and stayed a step away for comfort.

The hostess placed us in a booth, him and me on opposite sides of the horseshoe booth. He had ordered for us gin and tonics, which was accompanied with giving a wad of cash to the hostess before I could object. She quickly darted toward the bar, happy to execute the accountant's demand in order for her to keep her inflated tip.

While exploring the thick and varied menu, I listened to my companions study the menu. The boyfriend was eager to explore the steak and lobster options, while my date vocalized his love for all things calamari. My stomach rolled in disgust as I searched the menu for its quickest and lightest options. When it came time to order, I selected the balsamic chicken salad with a glass of white wine while my companions embraced more sophisticated options. My friend chose a personal great-white-shark pizza and a salad while our male companions ordered rib-eye steaks, two lobster tails, two orders of calamari, and a pitcher of beer.

For being invited to this double date, my role of outsider became solidified through their conversations and topics. While the three of them discussed memories and hot topics from their personal lives, I sat in relative silence, consumed my alcohol and complimentary chips and salsa in relative silence, chuckled when it was socially acceptable to do so, and nodded when my friend nodded in order to look somewhat interested in their mundane conversation. Whenever I interjected to participate, I'd receive awkward glances from the boys and a complete dismissal of my response as they continued to engage in conversation. My gaze actively shifted from the television above my date's head, which was showing live footage of the basketball game we were missing, to the activity at the kitchen, hoping to identify a lull in movement so that I could escape through the kitchen doors.

What distressed my stomach further than these exclusive and uncomfortable conversations was watching my male companions eat. While I am not a woman who is known for my table etiquette, I at least know the importance of maintaining social norms when I consume food. Eating as if they had starved for forty days in the desert, they ate and drank while showing no concern for the others around them. As they belched and farted as they pleased, my stomach struggled to hold down the crisp and sweet balsamic chicken that topped my colorful and flavor-packed salad. With desperate eyes, I gestured toward the waiter and requested the check and for it to be split into four ways.

"Whoa, whoa!" the boyfriend said, his greasy hands gesturing for the waitress to wait before she split the check. "I think it's time to discuss the importance of feminism in society."

Rolling my eyes with irritation, I asked, "What about feminism?"

"See, we don't live in a time when we need to be shackled to social norms about who pays for who on a date, ya know what I'm saying?"

"No, I don't," I replied, taking a calculated sip of wine while staring at the dirty man.

"See, I was raised to be a gentleman—pay for bitches, open doors—ya know, chivalry bullshit. But now I have been with my lady for years, and years of paying for dinners add up, ya know what I am saying?"

I took a glance at my friend, who began shrinking into her boyfriend's embrace while quietly reaching into her purse for her wallet. Knowing she was going to quiet her partner down by paying for his excessively extravagant and expensive meal, I shook my head and grabbed the bill from the waitress.

"Seeing as I don't know who the fuck you are, I can only judge by what I am seeing in front of me. And from what I can tell, without meaning any offense, you are a stereotypical, lazy piece of shit."

While choking on his gin and tonic, my date looked at me, shocked.

"You see, I didn't want to come out here this evening. However, your girlfriend told me that I would have a good time—enjoy my first NBA game, meet a nice guy, and enjoy her company. I expected to be accompanied by a gentleman whose love for basketball could help me stay focused throughout a game that I don't know very much about. Instead, your friend has been Silent Bob and would rather stare at the blinding sun than talk to me! Not only are we not at the game, thanks to your piss-poor planning and organization, but I am disgusted with every fiber of my being and may never eat again after watching the two of you consume your dinner. So if you think I am paying a dime for your mess, you are sorely mistaken. And if you have an ounce of self-respect, you will be paying for my friend's dinner because she deserves more than your sloppy and foul-mouthed demeanor."

An uncomfortable silence fell upon the table; the staring contest between me and my friend's boyfriend became the focus of the social interactions. With a game of chicken, he and I set the tone for how the closing of the evening would unfold. As the seconds drew out longer and longer, the waitress shifted her feet with discomfort.

"So the bill—"

"Split it into four, please, and thank you," I replied, my gaze not moving from the man across from me.

"You got it," she replied, and then she ran to divide the bill before an explosion of napkins and condiments burst from our table.

Losing the game of chicken that we began, he shook his head and gestured toward his girlfriend. "You had to pick a white bitch."

"Baby—"

"Nah, baby, you done and fucked up again. I swear, her brain in her head, ya know what I'm saying?" He motioned toward his friend.

"Excuse me?!" I said, shaking my head in disbelief.

I threw down two twenties; I was overpaying but was willing to eat the cost in order to escape this exchange. Getting up, I gathered my things and looked at my ghost of a friend with a sad smile. "Text me when you leave this loser."

"Nah, she won't be getting back to you! She is never gonna do better than me."

After walking out of the restaurant, I felt my anger turn into a disappointment laced with mourning and sadness. It was so hard for me to believe that such foul men existed, and I wasted my evening while being surrounded by their incompetence.

"Rach! Wait!"

To my surprise, the awkward accountant followed me outside. While shuffling his hands in his pockets, he stood before me. "Hey, I just want to apologize."

"It's a little too late for that," I responded sharply.

"Nah, girl. I get it. It was not our best performance. I am sorry for my part in this. Can I at least walk you to your car?"

I studied him with a skeptical glance; his aura radiated submission, and his honey-brown eyes were apologetic. With a heavy sigh, I conceded and allowed him to walk me to my car.

As I grabbed my keys, he took out his wallet and pulled out forty dollars. "Here." He took my empty hand in his and placed the bills there. "You came here tonight expecting a date, and we didn't provide that. I am sorry for my role in this."

"Thank you. I appreciate that." I nodded and gave his hand a squeeze of assurance.

I noticed his eyes widen, his pupils dilating, and his head nodding with more purpose and acceptance. As I turned to leave, he gripped my hand more firmly and turned my body to meet his. With bruising force, he stole my lips for a kiss, one hand firmly gripping my hand while the other pinned me to my driver's side door.

Annoyed and completely fed up with this mess of an evening, I shoved him off me forcefully. "What the fuck, dude?!"

"Mean—I kind of dig it," he replied before making his way to touch me again.

Instead, I took a step forward and pivoted away from my car. His gin-filled body wasn't prepared for my movement, and his body crashed into my side mirror before crashing onto the ground. "Ah, my bad!"

"Are you serious?!" I shouted in anger.

"Girl, we really ain't gonna fuck?" he asked, standing up and brushing himself off.

Before I could calm myself down and prepare a dignified answer, my right hand formed a fist, and I punched him directly in his nose. With a yell, he groaned and moved away from the door to a nearby tree.

"Nah," I replied sarcastically.

I quickly got into my Mountaineer and fled the parking lot as if my pants were on fire. The I-5 was the first welcome sight that I saw in hours.

The radio seemed to know that my evening wasn't filled with the romance and sparks of adventure that I had hoped for when my friend proposed the idea of a belated Valentine's Day date. Instead, the radio teased me with Pat Benatar's "Love Is a Battlefield" and Tanya Tucker's "Down to My Last Teardrop" to remind me that I was once again alone during another Hallmark holiday.

While I was bummed and disgusted after the evening's events, I was also showered with a sense of relief. While I was returning to my Baileys and ice cream, I didn't have to settle for those who didn't see me for the Valentine that I truly am. Valentine's may be for schmucks, but at least I'm not a schmuck.

XXIV: WHISKEY PRINCESS

Everyone chooses their poison,
The alcohol that enhances the color of their day-to-day personality
To buff out the scratches of life
Presenting a vibrant and boundaryless beauty
A charisma driven gentlemen
A comedian that rivals Robin Williams and Billy Crystal
Or the seductress that would give Sophia Loren a run for her
money.

I know the potions that release me of my chains
That unlock the structures that keep my Type A self in check
I also know that elixir will unleash the demons of vengeance and
destruction that patiently wait for their prey to approach.

You may have seen me embrace my Mexican heritage
Absorbing the comforts of Tequila, Agave and Lime,
The indulgence of margaritas and tequila shooters
Producing buried accents, unrivaled confidence and the clumsy
removal of clothes.
If I knowingly participate in the consumption of this potion,
I purposely wear multiple layers,
For I know they will be removed as the night rolls on.

Sugars are not my friend, as I have come to discover
The sweetness of rums and flavored alcohols
Leave my stomach rolling in displeasure
My skin turning a vibrant red tone
An illness brought about by Slovakian blood and Montero body heat.

Shall we crack open the clay jugs of luxurious wine,
Red rivers of comfort and sensuality
Poured into each glass,
Their legs becoming tangled vines on the glass after consumption.
With each sip, I slip deeper into the role of reasoning and rationalization
A woman who justifies the mistakes of men, yet ignores the many errors I have made myself.

No, we shall not visit the transparent enemy known as Vodka,
That Russian bastard,
Oh how you anger me so.
Your liquid so harsh and brutalizing,
You awaken a part of me that is calculating and deceptive,
A personality who seeks pleasure from seeing others hurt as much as I have,
Yet will deny it with the passion and conviction of martyrs and activists who have died for their causes,
My cause typically a lie that can distract others from seeing me and my broken heart.

You're in luck!
For you are having drinks with the Whiskey Princess tonight.
The amber liquid introduces you to a more relaxed version of myself,
A woman confident in her conversation with you,
Who meets you with a laundry list of expectations and desires,

Yet will only disclose those wants as the heartwarming magical elixir heats her core.

I can be the life of the party!

I don't need anything to chase it down

Only your lips, your tongue, your blood if I desire.

As the Whiskey Princess, I need to be adored and complimented,

Don't take my denial of your words as a rejection,

I'm wet from how badly you want me.

You'll notice my eyes are shifting

The amber moving away to a broken emerald.

Take your shot, I am yours tonight,

In the company of royalty you shall be.

XXV: X's and "Oh No's" (RK Arts)

XXVI: You Are a Queen

"You need to meet him."

I looked at my dear friend, startled by her sudden proclamation. I went to her apartment after she texted me, asking for remedies for her thrown-out back. With over a decade of experience of fixing my achy and eternally broken shoulder, I know what tricks are necessary to return to form when your body doesn't want to cooperate.

I was rubbing her back with warm olive oil, sea salt, and an essential oil of her choice for fragrance. I am always partial to ocean or mountain fragrances while my dearest favors the tropical and citrus varieties.

"What?" I asked; I rubbed my hands together to generate heat before returning them to her tweaked back.

"You need to go to him—my healer," she replied, her body giving in to my touch as I pressed further into the knot by her left hip.

Her healer was a kind man that she was referred to who would support her and guide her through the rainbow of emotions that she felt throughout her dynamic life. She was so much braver than me to be able to talk about every little element that she felt.

"I think I'm okay."

"Babe, you haven't had a full night's sleep in over a week. I know he had no way of knowing, but you have been triggered, babe."

My jaw clenched tightly, and I began inhaling deeply through my nose in order to suffocate the defensive words at the end of my tongue. I didn't want to think about that encounter. She was right.

I hadn't been resting—not completely. *I can't ignore how much he was like . . .*

"Consider this an early Christmas gift. Meet with him. See if he can unlock the box in your chest. Maybe he can help."

I am a decent avoider. In front of a crowd, I appear to be connected to my emotions and be able to identify how I feel about myself. Yet it is all a facade. If I am in a position to identify my own feelings and reactions, all I want to do is run.

As my thoughts ran wild, she must have felt my hands tense up. She removed herself from beneath my hold and looked at my distant amber eyes. She rubbed my wrist gently, making me return to her gaze. "You deserve a night's sleep that's not haunted by the past. Let me call him. See if he can help you get through this."

I agreed silently as she swiftly grabbed her teal cell phone and began making contact with this healer. From what I gathered from her, he was a kind and peaceful man who was strong with chi energy. His focus was on identifying and conquering traumatic events, particularly for women.

While she was leaving him a voice message, I couldn't deny that I was intrigued by this shaman. For years, I felt a wall of burden and pain build within my heart. As the losses of loved ones and lovers began to reach excessively high numbers, this metallic weight began anchoring itself in my chest cavity, each breath becoming more challenging to take.

Recently, I had my most severe anxiety attack. It left me nearly paralyzed on my couch, my muscles locked in unbearably painful positions and my chest muscles constricting against my ribs and lungs, making the intake of oxygen nearly impossible. With the heroic and loving support of my sisters, they were able to release me from my panicked prison with the aid of tequila and whiskey.

Then there was the incident—the encounter that dredged up nearly a decade of historical pain that I had convinced myself that I had conquered and abandoned. Since I was with him, my dreams were haunted by another figure—an angry and more vicious ghost from my past. My nights were plagued with cruel words and taunting statements that riddled my dreams with anguish. My engagements with the ghost of my mind would end in violence that would leave me choking for air or obliterated from graphic accidents. I'd wake up, unable to return to sleep, sweat cloaking my body and blood dripping onto my bedsheets. I would often turn on myself in the night, my fingernails ripping apart my back, arms, and legs. Late-night showers would cleanse my aching form as I scrubbed my body of the demons it fought in the night.

As my friend spoke of her experience with the healer, I couldn't help but wonder if there would be an opportunity to discuss these terrors in my mind. Maybe he would simply know the horrors that my dreams inflicted upon me from the dark circles beneath my eyelashes. As I prepared to explore this opportunity, I said a silent prayer, praying that this person could help me. It had been too long since I released this burden. I prayed that he would guide me through it or at least give me the universal signals I needed to go toward the right direction.

Nearly two weeks later, my day to meet with the healer had come. I had spent the earlier part of the day at Children's Hospital Los Angeles, making my platelet donation, which I had scheduled for every two weeks. It was a way that I could give back to those in my community that was unique and fit my broke budget. If I couldn't donate financially, I could at least provide my blood and platelets.

Being depleted of platelets provides me an odd rush throughout my day. Unlike the rush I get from my venti quad-shot espresso or the ease I gain from a long sip of old zinfandel, my mind and body are in a place of complete openness and ease after a donation session. As the minutes turn into hours, I feel a tingling sensation in my servicing arm as my own fluids pass through strategic pathways in a rocking motion of giving and receiving its own life force. While I am covered in multiple blankets and heated plastic bags to maintain my body temperature, my face and mouth always feel cold, the dryness of my lips being relieved with apple-berry juice and laughs from the incredible hospital staff.

It was after a three-hour donation session that I made my way toward this healer. He had shared that I needed to be in a place of openness and calm in order to allow our meeting to be beneficial. I never feel as calm and peaceful as I do after my donations. Making my way to Santa Monica didn't provide me anxiety or stress. Instead, I allowed myself to become mentally focused and somewhat prepared for what could happen with this interesting man.

When I arrived at the unit, I took a few moments to walk around the neighborhood and prepare myself for our session. I have always struggled with my emotions. I tend to turn to defensive measures and shut down when I feel cornered. From what my friend told me, this healer did not come from a place of judgment or ridicule. Yet the clenching of my jaw and the rubbing of my hands allowed my anxiety to produce doubts at the forefront of my mind.

I approached the apartments with caution and curiosity. Along my path was a small gray rabbit and a brown squirrel sharing their curious gaze toward me and a pinecone in the walkway. As I moved to avoid their interaction, I expected these creatures to run for the bushes. Instead, they moved beside me and guided me to the stairway.

Fifteen steps. Each of the steps was adorned with a welcoming idol or figurine that oddly eased my darting mind. The squirrel rushed to my right side while the rabbit waited at the bottom of the staircase. I knocked upon the blue-gray door gently, and I was greeted with a kind smile and warm eyes. He was slightly taller than me and held a stance of openness and confidence. I let out a sigh of relief as I introduced myself to him.

"I appreciate that your friends walked me to the door," I noted, turning toward the furry creatures.

"What do you mean?" he asked.

"These aren't yours?" I asked, motioning to the squirrel and the rabbit.

"No, they sure aren't," he replied. A humorous grin brightened his face as he looked out the door. When he made his way to the doorway, my native ushers scurried away from sight and into the brush. I chuckled and followed the healer into his home, wondering how the small critters knew where to guide me.

His home was full of color and peaceful energy. Surrounded by visuals promoting tranquility, energy, and healing, I found my defenses lowering with each passing moment. We sat at his kitchen table, which had bowls of exotic fruits and relaxing candles. His presence was one of comfort and unity. Living in Los Angeles for as long as I had, it had been such a long time since I had encountered a stranger who wasn't wound up and full of draining intensity.

He offered me water and nodded knowingly when I pulled out my liter bottle from my purse. I said that I needed to stay hydrated in order for my body to adjust from its lack of platelets. He asked me where my passion for donating platelets specifically came from. I opened up about the untimely passing of one of my former students, a shining baseball star whose short presence on our earth impacted the lives of thousands. As I told his brave story, I found tears escaping my eyes and my hands shaking in need to wipe away the evidence of my emotions. The healer was kind and shared that it was okay for me to release some of the pressure I had built within my chest due to grief and loss.

Quietly I nodded in agreement and began listening to everything this man wanted to share regarding his practice. As he spoke, I felt my heart rate slowing down, my mind becoming more accepting to his practices and strategies. Being honest with myself, I wanted to delve into this healing. For too long I felt isolated in my own heart and life. I came prepared to do what this healer could teach me.

We began by summarizing who I was and some areas of concern that I had regarding my current state of emotional health. I didn't know anything regarding emotional regulation and assessment for myself. I knew how to support and care for others. Being aware of one's emotional status seemed like a luxury meant for the privileged and underscheduled. He provided me an amiable smile in response and began sharing his belief in developing a personal emotional yoga, a methodology that allows each person to promote self-care and build upon our own abilities that make us better versions of ourselves.

He tenderly asked about my romantic life. I chuckled and shared that my romantic life had recently become a lesser priority due to a poor interaction with a potential partner. I could feel nervous energy traveling to my fingers, my need to wring my hands and rub my chest becoming primal and necessary.

"Do you feel comfortable with talking about your recent encounter?"

"Sure," I automatically responded. "This man is funny, bright, and full of life. He seems to be certain about everything. He isn't typically someone that I'd date. I don't typically go for talkers. Things seemed to be going smoothly. Then I went to pick him up from the airport."

"What happened there?" he asked.

"He was radically different from the man I dropped off. He was irritable. He seemed angry. Everything I did seemed to displease him. Then, as we were driving, we got caught up in 405 traffic." I paused, mentally reconstructing the puzzle pieces of our encounter in my mind. "It was so odd, and there was no way he could have known them, but he made some bitter comments that came directly from the mouth of my first love."

"Do you mind sharing what he said?"

I could feel a wedge of burning tears beginning to gather within my throat; fear of judgment and shame began to wrap my lungs in a suffocating blanket. "He said, *'I did this for you'*—meaning that he scheduled his flight to help me in picking him up. With the way the words came out of his mouth, he sounded exactly like the person who hurt me the most. From the second the words escaped him, I could feel my heart tightening within my chest. With a cautious turn of my head, I looked to the passenger seat and wanted to scream as he transformed into a person I hadn't seen in nearly ten years. I could no longer hear the words coming from his mouth. I only felt the intense pressure of fear and memory within my mind, pulsing and echoing within my eardrums."

"That is terrifying," the healer noted quietly, bringing me back from the painful memory.

I looked down and saw my hands holding my black dress tightly, my jean jacket burning my arms as I wanted to flee from my skin. "May I please take off my jacket?" I asked quickly.

"Of course. Please drink some water too if you need it."

I took off my jacket and placed it in my bag. After reaching for the water bottle, I allowed the cool liquid to ease the burn in my throat and calm me in front of the healer. It was too soon for me to look like a complete lunatic to this peaceful man.

"I don't blame him," I whispered. "There is no statistical way that he and the man from my past could have ever crossed paths. Maybe it was the universe sending me a blunt sign that I needed to step away from him."

The healer nodded and then took a moment to stand up. He began looking for an unknown item. His movements were full of rapid intent. After opening the cupboard by the hallway, he returned with a sheet of paper. Upon it were visuals that displayed a foundation for emotional healing and purposeful energy. He began sharing with me the importance of passion and discipline. Through the proper recognition of both aspects of ourselves, those two elements allow us to feel emotions more vividly. It is through self-care that we begin to identify emotions within ourselves, accept them as they are, and permit them to heal the brokenness within us.

We began his exercises, and I found myself becoming more open with each passing second. Through the sharing of tears and confessions, I was able to more accurately assess my life and the acidic box of heartbreak that was placed upon my chest.

It was during a twist of the emotion-filled process that the healing became more evident. The healer gave me a gentle motion toward my water bottle, silently reminding me to stay hydrated. As I was drinking, he asked me to identify a memory from my first love that held the most positive and healthy display of our love. Surprised by his request, I took a moment to delve into the file cabinet of memories in my mind and gave him a reminiscent grin as I shared a moment of spontaneity and romance from my younger years.

He had been craving a clam-chowder bread bowl after one of our evening classes. In a romantic rush, we left the college campus in his truck and drove straight to San Francisco. After two hours, we arrived at the Fisherman's Wharf and enjoyed an evening of quiet laughter and intimacy. As I told the story, I could feel his large hand encompassing mine as we searched for the seals upon the shore. I could still taste the warm mocha with cinnamon powder upon the whipped cream that filled my spirit with as much warmth as the boy beside me did. We were both exhausted and surprised that we were hours away from home during finals week, yet we couldn't have been happier just from being alone together in a different place. It was truly the peak of our time together.

I couldn't erase the smile on my face as the healer brought me back to the present. He asked me calmly and directly if I still felt love for this person even though he caused me so much pain. I needed a second to correctly answer his question. While our relationship was toxic and unhealthy, I couldn't deny that rehashing his memory in a positive way wasn't as horrible as I had anticipated. To be honest, I hadn't viewed him positively in years. He had been the first to break my innocence—the one who destroyed the fairy-tale vision I held for my romantic future. I blamed him for my defenses and my need to run from intimacy. I allowed the worst parts of him to become demons in my nightmares and taunt me into running from new men who crossed my path.

Yet, as pointed out by this healer, our time together wasn't completely dreadful. No, there was beauty in the chaos. The healer's question returned to my mind. After taking a breath, I responded, "I don't feel ill will for him anymore. The innocent love that I had felt for him has long since died. However, I only wish him happiness now."

"When your newest romantic partner scared you, how did you react?" the healer asked.

Focusing my mind on the brown-eyed brunet instead of the blue-eyed blond, my mind shifted to the recent drive that sparked the night terrors laced with cruel words and violence. "I shut down."

"What would you have done back then?"

"I would have blamed myself. I would have apologized and done anything for him to stay." The honesty that escaped my lips shocked me to my core. I could feel a small weight lift from my chest, my shoulders relaxing in a shuddering breath as new oxygen greeted my muscles.

"Is it possible that this car ride, while unpleasant and sparking traumatic nightmares and memories from your past, was a challenge from a guardian angel or the universe to see how far you have come since you were the woman you once were?"

His question challenged me in the most brilliant way. The phrasing of his words provided me a moment of realization and growth. Yes, my mind may still hold the memories of pain and devastation. However, the choice I made since then to now was much different. In my youth, my fear of loneliness and isolation made me panicked and desperate. Now, while I was still terrified of what could be, I allowed myself to stay strong on the outside and break down only within my dreams. After taking a deep breath, I felt the tears fall from my eyes as I recognized the progress I had made. I was no longer the woman I was then. I was evolving. I was improving. I was healing.

My conversation with the healer continued to explore various emotions that harnessed great energy within me. Through meaningful breathing exercises and mindful questions, I allowed myself to confront my ever-present opinions regarding emotions of shame and of bliss. With each coached breath, I could feel the weight upon my chest lightening. Gratitude and peace took the places of anxiety and fear.

We had moved to a table within the living room. I lay upon my back as he began a practice to release the toxic energy within me and begin healing the broken pieces within my spirit through breaths of love and self-care. His chanting included verbal intentions for security and openness—a combination that I had never imagined before. The healer explained that each breath I took in had the purpose of approaching the emotions of pain and anguish within me. With each exhalation, I was to forgive myself for the crimes I committed within my mind and heart. With each breath, I could feel my shoulders relaxing, the weight of my hair becoming lighter as he applied pressure to my neck and spine.

His tone shifted as he interrupted his chants to ask me a question: "When you engage with men, do you try to fix them?"

Taken by surprise, I replied, "I tend to try and fix everyone in my life. I'm a fixer by nature."

He placed his hand upon my forehead, and I could feel the raw heat of his palm. In a tone much deeper than his casual voice, he declared, "You are a queen. It is your time to be adored."

I opened my eyes and saw that his eyes were closed; his breaths were purposeful.

"You have loved, you have nurtured, and you have been strong for too long. It is time for you to find someone who will take care of you."

His words held assurance and certainty that I couldn't separate myself from. His hand moved away from my forehead and began stroking my hair with purposeful compassion. "You are a queen. It is time."

It was with his final declaration that my exhaling breath broke the metallic burden that was trapped in my chest. With a sigh, I could feel shards of pain and memory disintegrating into a deep-gray powder within my lungs. The inhaling breath I took moved with purpose to wrap itself around this shaking form. As I exhaled, the powder went through my esophagus and escaped my mouth in a moan of release that was tired from years of strain.

After a few moments of intentional healing, he left me alone so I could process what had happened. My mind and heart were no longer racing and were connected and still like the peaceful Serene Lakes up in Donner Pass. There was so much to absorb from this encounter. I was no longer afraid. I was no longer defensive. I was beginning to embrace openness and self-forgiveness. I was ready to heal and be better.

We exchanged good-byes as I expressed my gratitude through a hug and quiet laughs. He shared with me suggestions for how I needed to take care of myself in the days to come. As I walked to my car, I could feel each molecule of air upon my skin, the salt-filled air of Santa Monica healing my spirit. Upon my head now rested a crown of water lilies and roses, my wavy blond hair resting upon my shoulders with precision and grace. The smile I held no longer rested upon a shaky foundation. Instead, my steps were grounded in a revived belief in myself and my worth.

I am a queen. It is my time.

XXVII: Zealots for the Majestic Fairy Tale, Listen Up!

Aye, I can't believe we are at the end of our journey, and I am coming to you without a happily ever after.

Wait, maybe I am wrong about that.

I have loved, laughed, and gained so much through these dating disasters. There have been many reasons to throw in the towel and say *"No more! I'm done! Ready to die alone, eaten by the neighborhood feral cats surrounded by rescue pups and odd figurines!"* However, as I write this section, I can't help but smile at the relentless romantic flame of hope within me, tired yet steadily allowing me to feel alive.

Now you might think I'm crazy for wanting to stay in the dating game until I find my perfect match. What I have gained from these years of trial and error is the knowledge that my perfect match does not exist. Rather, the best match for me is indeed out there. While I adore my familia for giving me such high expectations for the men in my life, I realize that trying to categorize the men I date into columns and checklists is unethical and truly robbing me of incredible and broken human moments.

Instead of having the man I date fit a predetermined mold of romantic and marriage success, I must take the leap and go down the road of love and life by their side. I have allowed my previous hurts and pains to create barriers that men would have to leap over and barrel through in order to catch a glimpse of my heart. All that did was tire them out and poison my cynical heart further as I watched their exhausted souls walk away from me.

As I shared previously, I had become so tired that I had convinced myself that my soul mate had died during the September 11 attacks. It was easier to imagine that my soul mate had died before we ever met rather than believe that he was wandering life alone as the pit of loneliness within me burned to a point of numbness and dark humor. It wasn't until I shared this morbid truth during a moment of liquid weakness to my best friend that I realized how truly fucked that idea was. Her compassionate tears for my dark heart helped me see that living a life that is content because of assumed death rather than attempts at love was robbing me of joy, of love, and of passion. While I appeared to accept her advice with minimal reaction, her wise words laced with brokenhearted compassion helped me see that I could have more, that I could be desired and wanted, and that, statistically, my soul mate did not perish during those tragic attacks.

I've also learned the lesson of not comparing myself to others when it comes to love. In my early twenties, I attended my cousin's wedding in a quaint town called Auburn. A beautiful summer wedding, it was filled with cheesy engagement videos for the guests' entertainment and just-sweet-enough, expensive cake. Our familia danced around me, intoxicated by the heightened emotions of love and eternal companionship during this dry affair. While putting on a smile, I kept my jaded feelings of genuine lasting relationships to myself, giving hugs and kisses to family and friends who were caught up in the promise of the newest couple beginning their path toward forever.

One of my youngest cousins, a beautiful ballerina captured in teenage form, came dancing toward me with smiles and hugs, her joy radiating through each strand of her hair. She turned to me and said that I would be next down the aisle as she giggled and returned to the dance floor. Not only was she very wrong about her prediction, but this little dove also found her prized soul mate. They even have a baby boy on the way.

During my most bitter years, I saw the happiness of others and wanted to crush it—not with violence but with sarcasm and eye rolls. Their photos that captured their moments of bliss would cause the yellow bile to rise up my throat. Nausea and a sore attitude would stay with me for hours on end. *What did they do so right to be so diabetically sweet? Where did I go wrong?* I would ask myself.

The lesson, produced through time and needed self-love, is that I couldn't rush my timeline to meet theirs because we are all on different journeys. Everything we do is an opportunity for a brand-new adventure. Every person we meet provides wisdom, humor, and a dash of hope to guide us on our journey. If I settled upon their paths, it would be a robbery for us both. There is no sense in envying others when we all have different destinies with love.

Now we are here, the close of our journey. My alphabet of romance isn't complete. However, that doesn't leave me troubled. Instead, it gives me a refreshed sense of purpose. During this comical reflection, I found more laughter than tears. As I continue to look for my ideal match in life, I know that those pieces of my past will give me the wisdom and humor that I will need to identify the man who will appreciate my presence.

Once upon a time, I believed that falling in love would feel like a lightning bolt, that I would be forever changed in the moment I met him, and that my life's purpose would be redefined and I would walk down a newly paved path while blinded by love and protected by the winged angels of fate.

No longer do I believe that falling in love feels like an earthquake. Instead, I hope it is as calm as the ocean on a clear day—a confidence given to me in an overwhelming moment of clarity and understanding. From across a crowded room, with the flip of his hair and a shy smile, I hope my heart stops for the smallest of moments and that a whisper from the other side of mortality enters my ear and says "There ya go, kid." From there, I can stop the worry, the second-guessing, and the doubt. From that moment on, with whatever would come down our paths, I would know I'd be his and he'd find his way to me. Through God and through love, we would find our way. My heart would stop its agonizing tirade of worst-case scenarios and ultimatums.

My mind goes to the classic Disney film *Beauty and the Beast*. In its production, the story begins and concludes with mosaic art pieces. It brings me enormous comfort knowing that my own love story is its own mosaic. Cracked, broken, and glued together with tears and blood, the colorful glass of my piece of art is reflected in my amber eyes, mannerisms, dark humor, and fractured words. As with all imperfect things, its beauty is determined by the experiences and degrees of depth that allow the visual representation to take hold and be ready for world view. I am now in a place where my personal romantic mosaic can be viewed, judged, criticized, and hopefully, loved. One day, my ideal match will appreciate the brokenness that was needed to stand before him in our shared moment, ready to take our walk together toward our own happily ever after.